AF270265

Praise for
Eucharistic Amazement

"What a beautiful journey, rich in Sacred Scripture and the witness of saints through the ages! Whatever your age, depth of learning or faith, Father Stice guides you to experience with childlike wonder Jesus' gift of the Holy Eucharist and to see with fresh eyes of faith this loving Gift meant to change your life."

—Most Reverend Joseph E. Kurtz,
Archbishop Emeritus of Louisville

"Every Eucharistic Revival needs to be rooted in Eucharistic amazement. Incorporating accessible insights from great saints and the liturgy itself, Father Stice opens accessible paths toward 'a sense of awe, love, and childlike trust in the goodness and power of the Eucharistic Christ, and a desire never to be parted from him.'"

—David D. Spesia, Executive Director,
USCCB Secretariat of Evangelization and Catechesis

"*Eucharistic Amazement* lives up to its title by rekindling awe for the tremendous gift of Christ's presence under the appearances of bread and wine. These reflections have encouraged me to more consciously prepare to receive special graces tied to the liturgical year."

—Sara Perla, The Catholic Project,
Catholic University of America

"With insightful reflections and some lessons from the saints, Father Stice reminds us of how we are unified and transformed by love in an encounter with the gift of the Real Presence of Jesus Christ in the Eucharist."

—Cardinal Wilton Gregory, Archbishop of
The Roman Catholic Archdiocese of Washington, DC

"We need a deep sense of 'Eucharistic amazement,' as Saint John Paul II would say, in order to taste the abundance of life that Jesus promised. However, we oftentimes suffer from 'Eucharistic numbness.' Father Randy's book helps to reduce that disconnect, so we can experience all that we're made for."

—Tanner Kalina, Catholic Evangelist, Cofounder of
the *Saints Alive* podcast on the Hallow app,
author of *Aching for Greatness*

"With unequaled ease and singular theological precision, Father Stice has written a most precious book. The author reminds us that we are created for the Eucharist, for communion with Jesus Christ, and how 'greatly we desire Him' (Saint Teresa of Avila). This classic is suited for both private edification and parish renewal. It is equally timely and timeless, necessary and most life-giving reading for every Christian. Enthusiastically recommended!"

—Rev. Emery de Gaál, PhD, Professor of Dogmatic
Theology, University of St. Mary of the Lake

"Father Randy interweaves the Catholic intellectual, liturgical, and theological tradition of ages with the practice of real saints and suggestions for concrete helpful practices by lay people today—thus engaging minds and moving hearts.

Eucharistic Amazement is depth and richness of content delivered with brilliant simplicity."

—Carmen Fernández Aguinaco, Former Multicultural Specialist of the Secretariat for Divine Worship, USCCB

"Of the many words used by Catholics to describe the Mass, 'amazing' may rarely be heard—unfortunately. But it is this Eucharistic 'amazement' that Saint John Paul II sought to enkindle in his last encyclical. Father Stice is thus in good company with his present work, and John Paul II would surely appreciate the book's eye-opening insights—as should all Catholics."

—Christopher Carstens, Editor, *Adoremus Bulletin*

"Father Randy brilliantly lifts us out of the tragic fog of Eucharistic confusion so we can clearly see Christ present in the here and now. This study provides a life-changing path for those seeking to discover the truth of God's amazing gifts to be found within our liturgy."

—Jimmy Dee, Director of Evangelization and Faith Formation, Tennessee Knights of Columbus; Vice Chairman, Board of the Catholic Men's Leadership Alliance/Heroic Men

"Wow—Father Randy Stice hit a home run with this enlightening, easy-to-read journey of the Real Presence of the Eucharist. Practical applications coupled with a plethora of references from the Bible and the saints allow readers a true opportunity to grow in their faith and nurture their Eucharistic amazement."

—Dickie Sompayrac, President, Knoxville Catholic High School; 2024 Recipient of the Lead. Learn. Proclaim. Award from the National Catholic Educational Association

"*Sacrosanctum Concilium*, Vatican II's *Constitution on the Sacred Liturgy*, charged those with pastoral duties to assist believers in achieving full, conscious, and active participation in the liturgy. Father Stice has taken up this duty admirably by helping Catholics explore the mysteries of the liturgy through the contemplative insights of saints and doctors throughout Church history—including John Chrysostom (d. 407), Augustine (d. 430), Pope Gregory the Great (d. 604), Teresa of Avila (d. 1582), and Faustina Kowalska (d. 1938). *Eucharistic Amazement* opens a door into the transhistorical nature of the liturgy that unites all of us with the communion of saints."

— Dr. C. Colt Anderson, Full Professor of Christian Spirituality, Fordham University

EUCHARISTIC
AMAZEMENT

EUCHARISTIC AMAZEMENT

Experience the Wonder of the Mass

FATHER RANDY L. STICE

FOREWORD BY LAWRENCE FEINGOLD

Pauline
BOOKS & MEDIA

Boston

Library of Congress Control Number: 2024932062

ISBN 10: 0-8198-9137-1

ISBN 13: 978-0-8198-9137-2

Art and design by www.kenjames.studio

Published by Pauline Books & Media, 50 Saint Pauls Avenue, Boston, MA 02130-3491

Printed in the U.S.A.

www.pauline.org

Pauline Books & Media is the publishing house of the Daughters of St. Paul, an international congregation of women religious serving the Church with the communications media.

1 2 3 4 5 6 7 8 9   29 28 27 26 25

Contents

Foreword

THE TOTAL GIFT OF himself that Christ gives us in the Eucharist ought to lead us "to profound amazement and gratitude," an amazement that should "always fill the Church," as Saint John Paul II says in his encyclical *Ecclesia de Eucharistia*.[1] John Paul II's goal in writing this Eucharistic encyclical is to "rekindle this Eucharistic 'amazement.'"[2] All of us need this rekindling, because we are all tempted to take for granted the riches we are given in the Eucharist.

The beginning of philosophy, according to Plato and Aristotle, is wonder, which is enkindled by reflecting on what transcends our understanding. This is even more true for theology. Theological wonder is caused by the gap between what our eyes see and the magnitude of what we recognize by our faith. Amazement in the power of the Eucharist led the martyrs of Abitene, who were arrested during the persecution of Diocletian for going to Sunday Mass, to say, "Without Sunday, we cannot live." Eucharistic wonder is nourished by growth in Eucharistic faith, which in turn needs to be nurtured by prayer rooted in sound catechesis and the faith of the saints. We encounter all of this abundantly in this admirable book by Father Randy Stice.

Eucharistic wonder begins with the Real Presence: Jesus is here with his entire personal being in every tabernacle, and we receive him—Body, Blood, soul, and divinity—in every Holy Communion. The sacrifice of the Mass is no less a source of wonder. Although we were born two thousand years too late to stand at the foot of the cross with Mary and John, Jesus instituted the Eucharist so that his paschal mystery can bridge the centuries to become mysteriously present in every Mass, enabling us to truly participate in his sacrifice today.

Chapter 4 speaks of the marvel that the faithful, through their royal priesthood, participate in their own way in offering Christ's sacrifice to God the Father, a sacrifice made present on the altar through the sacramental words of the ministerial priest acting in the person of Christ. The faithful participate in Christ's sacrifice by offering themselves and their loved ones with him, for we are a part of his Body. The Second Vatican Council, in its document on the priesthood, says that "priests must instruct their people to offer to God the Father the Divine Victim in the Sacrifice of the Mass, and to join to it the offering of their own lives."[3] How many of the faithful have learned this from their priests? Father Stice takes this responsibility seriously, and he helps the faithful to follow the teaching of *Sacrosanctum Concilium*:

> The Church, therefore, earnestly desires that Christ's faithful, when present at this mystery of faith, should not be there as strangers or silent spectators; on the contrary,

through a good understanding of the rites and prayers they should take part in the sacred action conscious of what they are doing, with devotion and full collaboration.... By offering the Immaculate Victim, not only through the hands of the priest, but also with him, they should learn also to offer themselves.[4]

Through the Mass we also come to participate in the mysteries of Christ's life that we celebrate in the liturgical year, as Father Stice explains in chapter 5. We are given graces to grow in longing for his coming in Advent, to be born anew with him at Christmas, to be transfigured with his transfiguration, to be vigilant in temptation, pray, fast, and do works of mercy with him during Lent, to rise with him to new life at Easter, and to be filled with the Holy Spirit with the apostles at Pentecost.

The best way to foster Eucharistic devotion is to look to Mary as the model of Eucharistic amazement. John Paul II ends *Ecclesia de Eucharistia* with a profound meditation on what it would have been like for Mary to participate in the Eucharist and receive her Son. Through Holy Communion the faithful receive in their bodies the same humanity of the Word that Mary received in her womb at the Annunciation and welcomed anew in every Holy Communion. Our "Amen" with which we receive him, like Mary's fiat, should express our wonder that the Creator, having become man, wishes to become present where we are and dwell in our bodies. Mary also exemplifies the sacrificial dimension of the Eucharist, as she offered her Son while standing at the foot of the cross on Calvary. What Mary offered then—her Son as the Divine

Victim to atone for the sins of the world—is offered by the Church in every Mass. Mary would have grown in grace and intimacy with her Son in an unparalleled way through every Holy Communion, as she received the Son whom she had nurtured in her womb and accompanied to Calvary. Let us ask Mary to help us to share in her Eucharistic life ever more deeply.

LAWRENCE FEINGOLD

NOTES

1. John Paul II, *Ecclesia de Eucharistia* (Boston: Pauline Books & Media, 2003), 5.

2. John Paul II, *Ecclesia de Eucharistia*, 6.

3. Vatican Council, *Presbyterorum Ordinis* (December 7, 1965), The Holy See, Vatican.va. 5 https://www.vatican.va/archive/hist_councils/ii_vatican_council/documents/vat-ii_decree_19651207_presbyterorum-ordinis_en.html.

4. Vatican Council, *Sacrosanctum Concilium* (December 4, 1963), The Holy See, Vatican.va, 48. https://www.vatican.va/archive/hist_councils/ii_vatican_council/documents/vat-ii_const_19631204_sacrosanctum-concilium_en.html.

Introduction

T HIS BOOK IS THE fruit of my personal path to discovering a sense of Eucharistic amazement. I was raised a Protestant and was first drawn to the Eucharist while teaching English and sharing the Gospel in Communist China. It was while there that I began to read Catholic classics and was especially influenced by *The Imitation of Christ* by Thomas à Kempis. The last section is on the Eucharist, and Thomas' emphasis on the Real Presence, the importance of holiness, and devout preparation started me thinking about the Catholic understanding of the Lord's Supper.

Sacred Scripture was key to my reflection on the Eucharist, especially the Bread of Life discourse in John 6. I was attracted by the intimate personal relationship Jesus promised: "Those who eat my flesh and drink my blood abide in me, and I in them" (Jn 6:56). These words of Jesus in John 6:53 struck me powerfully: "Unless you eat the flesh of the Son of Man and drink his blood, you have no life in you." I remember thinking to myself that this was not something that I wanted to be wrong about!

At the time I was particularly drawn to two Catholic figures, Saint John Paul II and Saint Teresa of Calcutta. Jesus' teaching on the Eucharist prompted probing questions: If Catholics were wrong and Protestants were right about the Eucharist, then where were the Protestant figures that command the same universal respect that these two Catholics do? And more than that, are John Paul II and Mother Teresa examples of the life imparted by Jesus through receiving the Eucharist? These questions challenged and unsettled me.

When the *Catechism of the Catholic Church* was published in 1994, I bought a copy, eager to compare what I had heard about the Eucharist growing up as a Protestant with what the Church actually taught. I was particularly persuaded by the biblical support for the Catholic understanding of the Real Presence. I also began to wonder: If the Catholic Church was wrong about its understanding of the Eucharist, why did God wait fifteen hundred years for the Protestant Reformation to correct it? I had no good answer to this question. I was attending an Episcopal church just prior to my reception into the Catholic Church. Before each service I meditated on a series of Bible passages on the Eucharist that I had assembled, including John 6:51, 53–56; First Corinthians 10:16; 11:28. Under the guidance of the Holy Spirit, these verses of Scripture as well as conversations with a local priest led me to faith in the Real Presence of Christ. I was received into the Catholic Church in 1997.

Over the next several years I attended Mass daily, continued to read and pray, and began to discern a vocation, first to religious life, and then to diocesan priesthood. I was accepted as a seminarian by the Diocese of Knoxville in the fall of 2002 and entered Mundelein Seminary in December of that year. During my first week I suffered two heart attacks four days apart, but I recovered and four years later was ordained a priest in June 2007. Later that summer I completed a Licentiate in Sacred Theology, writing my thesis on Saint Teresa of Avila. I was appointed the Director of the Office of Worship and Liturgy in 2009 and earned an MA in Liturgy from the Liturgical Institute in 2011. After serving as an associate pastor and pastor, I worked at the USCCB in the Secretariat of Divine Worship from 2017 to 2020, after which I retired and returned to Knoxville.

Priesthood has only deepened my love and awe for the Eucharistic Christ. The celebration of the Mass, the highlight of each day, continually deepens my personal encounter with Jesus in the Eucharist. Offering Mass for a variety of groups—parishes, religious communities, different cultural and language groups, Catholic school students from elementary to high school, USCCB staff, pilgrimages—has helped me see new ways in which our Eucharistic Lord offers himself to all. My appointment as the diocesan director of liturgy gave me the opportunity to read, reflect, write, and teach about the Mass, further enriching my experience of the Eucharist as an encounter with the Trinity. Every day I say with the Apostle Paul, "Thanks be to God for his indescribable gift!" (2 Cor 9:15)

I conceived the idea for *Eucharistic Amazement* while preparing a homily for the feast of Saint John Neumann (January 5). The prayers for the Mass—the Collect, the Prayer over the

Offerings, and the Prayer after Communion—struck me with their petition that we experience *the power of the sacrament*, a phrase that, with slight variations, occurs over fifty times in the Roman Missal. Very quickly I had formulated an outline for a book on the Eucharist that would bring together my experience in the field of liturgy with my work on Saint Teresa of Avila, my devotional reading of Saint Faustina's *Diary*, my interest in the Eucharistic writings of Saint John Chrysostom, and Pius Parsch's discussion of what he called the "peculiar" graces of each celebration of the Mass.

This book will take you on a journey. In Chapter 1 we will begin by reflecting on Christ's personal and powerful Presence in the Eucharist and study several examples of the Eucharistic amazement of Christians down through the centuries. Chapter 2 explores the relationship between Christ's earthly ministry and his action in the Mass, as well as the importance of faith, knowledge, and love in our participation in Mass. Saint Teresa of Avila, in Chapter 3, shares the graces of her encounters with Christ in the Eucharist, which will lead to a discussion in Chapter 4 of how we encounter the Trinity in the Mass, focusing on the renewal of the Covenant in the Mass.

The specific way in which God makes present the specific graces of each liturgical season and feast of the liturgical year is the subject of Chapter 5. Two liturgical pioneers will lead the way in this study, followed by Pope Pius XII, the teaching of the Second Vatican Council, and the *Catechism of the Catholic Church*. To illustrate this teaching, in Chapter 6 we will be guided once more by a saint, this time by Saint Faustina Kowalska, the Apostle of Divine Mercy, who shares her experience of the graces of the different seasons and feasts of the liturgical year. In Chapter 7 we delve more deeply into the parts of the Mass and reflect on how we can prepare ourselves to receive the unique graces of each liturgical celebration. In Chapter 8, we turn to the compelling witness of the Doctor of the Eucharist, Saint John Chrysostom, concluding in Chapter 9 by pondering what it will mean for our whole life to be transformed by Eucharistic amazement.

The purpose of this book is for you to cultivate a sense of Eucharistic amazement, primarily by presenting the teaching of the Church and the saints on the Eucharist. However, we are transformed when this information is combined with experience. For this reason, in the sections Nurturing Eucharistic Amazement which you will find in each chapter, I suggest practical applications of the material, ways in which you can put what you have read into practice either in preparation for Mass, during Mass, or after Mass, to deepen your own spirit of Eucharistic amazement.

Finally, a note on sources for the Fathers of the Church quoted in this book. In general, quotations are taken from primary sources, but I've made two exceptions. Wherever possible I have chosen to use material from Church Fathers as quoted in sources such as a papal document or the *Catechism of the Catholic Church*, because referencing such magisterial sources indicates the enduring value of the teaching of the Fathers and also provides a consistent approach to the mysteries of our faith.

Abbreviations

EE   *Ecclesia de Eucharistia (On the Eucharist in Its Relationship to the Church)*, John Paul II, 2003.

CCC   *Catechism of the Catholic Church*, 2nd ed., 1995.

LF   *Lumen Fidei (On Faith)*, Francis, 2013.

MD   *Mediator Dei (On the Sacred Liturgy)*, Pius XII, 1947.

MF   *Mysterium Fidei (On the Holy Eucharist)*, Paul VI, 1965.

SC   *Sacrosanctum Concilium (Constitution on the Sacred Liturgy)*, Second Vatican Council, 1963.

SacCar *Sacramentum Caritatis (On the Eucharist as the Source and Summit of the Church's Life and Mission)*, Benedict XVI, 2007.

VD   *Verbum Domini (On the Word of God in the Life and Mission of the Church)*, Benedict XVI, 2010.

CHAPTER 1

Does God Act Today?

And so all that the Son of God did and taught for the world's reconciliation is not for us simply a matter of past history. Here and now we experience his power at work among us.

SAINT LEO THE GREAT, *SERMON XII ON THE PASSION*

THE APOSTLE PAUL FIRST preached the Gospel to the Thessalonians in the face of serious opposition and their acceptance of the Gospel came with great suffering. They persevered, however, despite continued persecution. In many parts of the world persecution is still a reality. To encourage the Thessalonians, and us, Saint Paul recalled for them their first experience of the Gospel. "Our message of the gospel," he wrote, "came to you not in word only, but also in power and in the Holy Spirit and with full conviction" (1 Thess 1:5). However, many today do not share Paul's certainty about the power of the Gospel to transform our lives and draw us into the love of the Trinity. In *The Light of Faith*, Pope Francis wrote, "Our culture has lost its sense of God's tangible presence and activity in our world. We think that God is to be found in the beyond, on another level of reality, far removed from our everyday relationships."[5] Even Christians can struggle to maintain a sense of God's presence and activity in the world. We too may believe that God only exists in a realm far from us. Although we know God exists, we may doubt his active and loving presence in our world, in our parish, and in our own lives.

What if it were true that God was not acting in the world? If this were true then his love would not be real or powerful, his promises would be meaningless, and our faith empty. This is certainly not the faith that Christ entrusted to his Church and that has been faithfully passed on through the centuries. Almost two thousand years ago Saint Paul reminded the Corinthians that "My speech and my proclamation were not with plausible words of wisdom, but with a demonstration of the Spirit and of power, so that your faith might rest not on human wisdom but on the power of God" (1 Cor 2:4–5). We believe in a God whose love is real and powerful, a God we can encounter, who is truly Emmanuel, "God with us" (see Mt 1:23), a God who is personally and powerfully involved in our world and in our lives.

There are many ways in which God acts in our world today. In this book we will consider specifically how God acts in the Mass, which is "a meeting of God's children with their Father, in Christ and the Holy Spirit."[6] The Second Vatican Council called the Eucharist "the source and summit of the

Christian life," in which Christ is present and acts in a number of ways: in the proclamation of Sacred Scripture (his word), in the assembly (his Body), in the priest (his minister), but "most especially in the Eucharistic species."[7] In the most Blessed Sacrament of the Eucharist, "Christ himself, living and glorious, is present in a true, real, and substantial manner: his Body and his Blood, with his soul and his divinity" (CCC 1413). Hidden under the appearances of bread and wine, Christ is personally present and continues to act today as he did during his earthly ministry.

I Am with You Always

The transformation of the bread and wine into the Body and Blood of Christ is both miracle and mystery, something that we can never fully comprehend and explain. For two thousand years the Church has diligently reflected on this mystery and has deepened her understanding of Christ's Eucharistic presence. We can summarize his Eucharistic presence in this way: the Eucharist is the *substantial* presence of Christ's *glorified Body* under the *appearances* of bread and wine discerned by *faith*. Let's look more closely at the four italicized terms that indicate four key aspects of Christ's presence in the Eucharist.

First, Christ's presence in the Eucharist is a *substantial* presence. Saint Paul VI explained that "the way in which Christ becomes present in this Sacrament is through the conversion of the whole substance of the bread into his Body and of the whole substance of the wine into his Blood." The

Church calls this "unique and truly wonderful conversion"[8] transubstantiation, the complete change of one substance into another substance. The result of this complete change of the substance of bread and wine into the Body and Blood of Christ is presence.

> This presence is called "real"—by which is not intended to exclude the other types of presence as if they could not be "real" too, but because it is presence in the fullest sense: that is to say, it is a *substantial* presence by which Christ, God and man, makes himself wholly and entirely present. (CCC 1374)

All that remains of the bread and wine are the *outward characteristics*—appearance, texture, and taste.

Furthermore, the substantial presence of Christ in the Eucharist is not his Body during his earthly ministry before the resurrection, but *his resurrected Body*. "The flesh of the Son of Man, given as food," explained Saint John Paul II, "is his Body in its glorious state after the resurrection."[9] To appreciate the significance of this, recall the Gospel accounts of Christ's resurrection appearances. Sometimes his disciples recognized him, but other times they did not. He wasn't a ghost or a spirit—he ate with them and he still bore the wounds from the crucifixion. However, he could also suddenly appear in a locked room. What these encounters convey is the mysterious yet powerful reality of Christ's resurrected and glorified Body. Through the centuries the Church has echoed Saint Paul's desire to know the power of Christ's resurrection (see Phil 3:10). Because the Eucharist is Christ's resurrected Body, wrote Saint John Paul II, "with the Eucharist we digest, as it were, the 'secret' of the resurrection" (EE 18).

Finally, Christ's presence in the Eucharist can only be discerned by *faith*, not by our senses. Our senses tell us that what we receive in the Eucharist is bread and wine. But our faith discerns the truth with absolute certainty, a faith that is based on the words of Christ: "This is my body," "This is my blood" (Mk 14:22, 24). The Church has always believed and taught this truth. Saint Cyril of Jerusalem (†386) instructed the new Christians, "Do not see in the bread and wine merely natural elements, because the Lord has expressly said that they are his Body and Blood; *faith assures you of this*, though your senses suggest otherwise."[10] Saint John Chrysostom (†407) encouraged his flock to trust the words of Christ:

> Let us submit to God in all things and not contradict him, even if what he says seems to contradict our reason and intellect; *let his word prevail over our reason* and intellect. Let us act in this way with regard to the Eucharistic mysteries, and not limit our attention just to what can be perceived by the senses, but instead hold fast to his words. For his word cannot deceive.[11]

A few decades later, Saint Cyril of Alexandria (†444) wrote, "Do not doubt whether this is true, but rather receive the words of the Savior in faith, for since he is the truth, he cannot lie."[12]

Christ's presence in the Eucharist is different from any other presence in the world. In the Eucharist he is "present . . . in a totally unique way. . . . Jesus is not present in the Eucharist as a 'thing' or an object, but as a person."[13] Christ's presence in the Eucharist, therefore, is a *personal* presence. In the Eucharist Christ fulfills the promise he made to the apostles, "I am with you always, to the end of the age" (Mt 28:20). In the Eucharist Christ is truly Emmanuel, God with us.

Eucharistic Amazement Through the Centuries

Christians throughout the ages have marveled at the power of Christ's personal presence in the Eucharist and have proclaimed it in poetry, in theology, and with their very lives. In the year 304, forty-nine Christians in the small village of Abitene in modern-day Tunisia were arrested one Sunday during Mass because they had defied the Emperor Diocletian's order forbidding the celebration of the Eucharist. When asked why they had disobeyed the Emperor, one of them replied, "Without Sunday, we cannot live." In other words, life without the Eucharist, without coming together on Sunday to celebrate the Mass, would be impossible. For their devotion to the Eucharist, these Christians of Abitene were tortured and martyred. These brave Christians, amazed at the power of the Eucharist they had experienced, placed the Eucharist at the very center of their lives.

In his autobiography *Confessions*, Saint Augustine (†430) described a personal experience of the transforming power of the Eucharist. Addressing God, he recalled the occasion when it seemed "as if I heard your voice from on high: 'I am the food of strong men; grow and you will feed on me; nor will you change me like ordinary food into your flesh, but you will be changed into me.'"[14] Commenting on this passage, Pope Benedict XVI wrote, "It is not the Eucharistic food that is changed into us, but rather we who are mysteriously transformed by it. Christ nourishes us by uniting us to himself; 'he draws us into himself.'"[15] This transformative power of the Eucharist is another source of amazement.

Saint Francis of Assisi (†1226) was so awestruck at the mystery of Christ's hidden presence that he broke into ecstatic poetry:

> Let the whole world tremble;
> let heaven exult
> when Christ, the Son of the Living God,
> is on the altar in the hands of the priest.
> O admirable height and stupendous condescension!
> O humble sublimity! O sublime humility!
> That the Lord of the universe,
> God and the Son of God,
> so humbles himself that for our salvation
> he hides himself under a morsel of bread.
> Consider, brothers, the humility of God
> and pour out your hearts before him.

Before the miracle of Christ's Eucharistic presence, a manifestation of his unfathomable humility, the world shakes, heaven exults, and we are moved to pour out our hearts to him.

The hymn *Adoro Te, Devote*, attributed to Saint Thomas Aquinas (†1274) and translated by the Catholic priest and poet Gerard Manley Hopkins, is a marvel of devotional theology.

> Godhead here in hiding, whom I do adore
> Masked by these bare shadows, shape and nothing more,
> See, Lord, at thy service low lies here a heart
> Lost, all lost in wonder at the God thou art.
>
> Seeing, touching, tasting are in thee deceived;
> How says trusty hearing? that shall be believed;
> What God's Son has told me, take for truth I do;
> Truth himself speaks truly or there's nothing true.

These eight lines explain the mystery of Christ's presence. "Godhead here in hiding"—the glorified Christ, united with the Father and the Holy Spirit, is hidden under the appearances of bread and wine, appearances which are "bare shadows, shape and nothing more." We cannot discern Christ's presence with our senses, for "seeing, touching, tasting are in thee deceived." Only "trusty hearing"—faith in the words of Christ—assures us of Christ's presence: "What God's Son has told me, take for truth I do; Truth himself speaks truly or there's nothing true."

Saint Thérèse of Lisieux (†1897), the Little Flower, marveled at the love of Jesus revealed in the Eucharist. "It is not to remain in a golden ciborium that he comes to us *each day* from heaven," she wrote, "it's to find another heaven, infinitely more dear to him than the first: the heaven of our soul, made to his image, the living temple of the adorable Trinity!"[16] In this one sentence Thérèse indicates something very important about God and about us. The Eucharist reveals to us the depth of God's love for us and his desire for relationship with us. And it reveals the immense dignity that God has bestowed on us: each of us, made in his image, is a living temple and a unique heaven that God desires to fill with his presence. Can anything testify more eloquently to the dignity that we have in God's eyes? Despite our frailty and brokenness, the Father, Son, and Holy Spirit want to make of our souls another heaven. This too enkindles in us an awe before the Eucharist.

Venerable Francis-Xavier Nguyen Van Thuan (†2002), a Vietnamese cardinal, offers a very different but equally compelling witness of Eucharistic amazement. On August 15, 1975, the feast of the Assumption, he was arrested by the Communist government of Vietnam and imprisoned for thirteen years. Through all those years, with wine and hosts that had been smuggled into the prison and using his hand for a chalice, he continued to celebrate Mass every day. He and his Catholic companions made small containers from cigarette packages in which they placed the Blessed Sacrament to share among the Catholic prisoners. "They all knew that Jesus was among them, he who could heal all their physical and mental suffering. At night, the prisoners took turns for adoration; Jesus helped us in a tremendous way with his silent presence."[17] Cardinal Van Thuan spent nine of his thirteen years in solitary confinement. The Masses he celebrated during those nine years he considers "the most beautiful Masses of my life."[18]

Fourth century martyrs in Abitene, an ancient bishop of North Africa (Saint Augustine), the founder of a religious order that exalted Lady Poverty (Saint Francis of Assisi), a young French Carmelite nun (Saint Thérèse of Lisieux), and a persecuted shepherd (Cardinal Van Thuan) have expressed with their words and their lives what Saint John Paul II called "Eucharistic 'amazement.'" Reflecting on the witness of these Christians, we can say that Eucharistic amazement is *a sense of awe, love, and childlike trust in the goodness and power of the Eucharistic Christ, and a desire never to be parted from him.* Saint John Paul II ardently desired that this amazement "should always fill the Church assembled for the celebration of the Eucharist" (EE 5).

Nurturing Eucharistic Amazement

Christians throughout the centuries have witnessed to their faith in the Eucharist by expressing *a sense of awe, love, and childlike trust in the goodness and power of the Eucharistic Christ and a desire never to be parted from him.* Here are some suggestions for cultivating, expressing, and sharing Eucharistic amazement in your own life.

- You may want to imitate Saint Francis of Assisi by composing a poem expressing your amazement.

- You may want to follow Saint Thomas Aquinas' example and write a hymn or song.

- Children (and adults) can share their amazement through a drawing or painting.

- Two of our examples, the Abitene martyrs and Cardinal Van Thuan and his companions, faced being deprived of the Mass. Considering their perseverance and our experience of the COVID pandemic, you may want to begin attending a weekday Mass in addition to the weekly Sunday Mass.

✦ For personal reflection: How does the Mass make a difference in your life?

———————————————————●———————————————————

Two Moments of Eucharistic Amazement in the Mass

The Mass itself forms us in this Eucharistic amazement especially during two moments: the Consecration and the Communion Rite. The Consecration is the moment when the bread and wine are transubstantiated into the Body and Blood of Christ. The priest first holds his hands over the bread and wine and calls down upon them the Holy Spirit, and then takes each into his hands while Jesus says through him—"This is my Body," "This is my Blood." While still a cardinal, Pope Benedict XVI wrote of this:

> The moment when the Lord comes down and transforms bread and wine to become his Body and Blood cannot fail to stun, to the very core of their being, those who participate in the Eucharist by faith and prayer. . . . The Consecration is the moment of God's great *actio* [action] in the world for us.[19]

The actions that accompany this moment express this amazement. The priest leads the assembly in worship, first raising the Host and showing it to the assembly (the elevation), then genuflecting in adoration. He does the same with the chalice.

Bells are often rung at this moment to signal the miracle that has just taken place, and at solemn celebrations the Body and Blood are incensed at the elevation.

The Communion Rite is another moment of Eucharistic amazement. It has always been accompanied by gestures and postures that express reverence and love, for in the words of Saint Augustine, "No one eats that flesh without first adoring it; we should sin were we not to adore it" (SacCar 66). Theodore of Mopsuestia (†428) told his congregation to approach the altar looking down: "By looking downwards you signify that you are offering God fitting adoration, and giving thanks for receiving the body of the King, who became the Lord of all through His union with the divine nature, and who is worshipped as a Lord by the whole creation."[20] In the sixth century monks approached Communion with prostration and genuflection, a practice that spread more widely in the tenth and eleventh centuries. Today we bow before receiving the Body and Blood of Christ because, explains Saint John Paul II, "If, in the presence of this mystery, reason experiences its limits, the heart, enlightened by the grace of the Holy Spirit, clearly sees the response that is demanded, and bows low in adoration and unbounded love" (EE 62).

Conclusion

Does God act in the world today? Indeed he does, and in an altogether unique way in the Mass. In the Eucharist we encounter Christ fully present as he is now, the glorified only-begotten Son of God, personally present yet hidden, perceived only by faith, powerfully active. Christians down the centuries have encountered Christ's transforming presence in the Eucharist and have left descriptions and explanations of their experiences that continue to instruct and encourage the Church's Eucharistic amazement. In the following pages we will explore how the Mass is a unique encounter with "God's tangible and powerful love which really does act in history and determines its final destiny" (LF 17).

NOTES

5. Francis, *Lumen Fidei* (Boston: Pauline Books & Media, 2013), 17 (hereafter cited in text as LF).

6. *Catechism of the Catholic Church*, 2nd ed. (New York: Doubleday, 1995), 1153 (hereafter cited in text as CCC).

7. Vatican Council, *Sacrosanctum Concilium* (December 4, 1963), The Holy See, Vatican.va, 7 (hereafter cited in text as SC). https://www.vatican.va/archive/hist_councils/ii_vatican_councildocumentsvat-ii_const_19631204_sacrosanctum-concilium_en.html.

8. Paul VI, *Mysterium Fidei* (September 3, 1965), The Holy See, Vatican.va, 46 (hereafter cited in text as MF). https://www.vatican.va/content/paul-vi/en/encyclicals/documents/hf_p vi_enc_0309 1965_mysterium.html.

9. John Paul II, *Ecclesia de Eucharistia* (Boston: Pauline Books & Media, 2003), 18 [Cyril of Jerusalem, *Mystagogical Catecheses*, IV, 6: SCh 126, 138] (hereafter cited in text as EE).

10. John Paul II, *Ecclesia de Eucharistia*, 15 [Cyril of Jerusalem, *Mystagogical Catecheses*, IV, 6: SCh 126, 138]. Italics added.

11. Paul VI, *Mysterium Fidei*, 17 [St. John Chrysostom, *Homily on Matthew*, 82.4; PG 58.743].

12. *Catechism of the Catholic Church*, 1381 [St. Thomas Aquinas, STh III, 75, 1; cf. Paul VI, MF 18; St. Cyril of Alexandria, In Luc. 22,19: PG 72, 912; cf. Paul VI, MF 18].

13. Raniero Cantalamessa, *The Eucharist: Our Sanctification*, rev. ed. (Collegeville: Liturgical Press, 1995), 82.

14. *Augustine of Hippo: Selected Writings*, trans. Mary T. Clark (New York: Paulist Press, 1984), 71.

15. Benedict XVI, *Sacramentum Caritatis* (Boston: Pauline Books & Media, 2007), 70 (hereafter cited in text as SacCar).

16. Thérèse of Lisieux, *Story of a Soul: The Autobiography of St. Thérèse of Lisieux*, 3rd ed., trans. John Clarke, O.C.D. (Washington, DC: ICS Publications, 1996), 104.

17. Francis-Xavier Nguyen Van Thuan, *Five Loaves and Two Fish* (Boston: Pauline Books & Media, 1997), 35.

18. Van Thuan, *Five Loaves*, 36.

19. Joseph Ratzinger, *The Spirit of the Liturgy* (San Francisco: Ignatius Press, 2000), 212.

20. Theodore of Mopsuestia, *Commentary of Theodore of Mopsuestia on the Lord's Prayer and on the Sacraments of Baptism and the Eucharist*. Translated by Alphonse Mingana. Woodbrook Studies 6, 1993. Public Domain.

CHAPTER 2

Power Came Forth from Him

Everything in him was full of sacraments, full of miracles.

SAINT LEO THE GREAT, *THE LETTERS AND SERMONS*

JESUS, SURROUNDED BY A crowd that was almost crushing him, was making his way to the home of a synagogue official to heal his daughter when a woman approached him.[21] She was ill, having suffered hemorrhages for twelve years, and she was desperate, for despite having spent all she had, the doctors had been unable to cure her. "She said to herself, 'If I only touch his cloak, I will be made well'" (Mt 9:21). She came up behind Jesus, touched his cloak, and was immediately healed. Jesus instantly knew it, saying to the apostles around him, "Someone touched me; for I noticed that power had gone out from me" (Lk 8:46). As Jesus looked around, the woman came forward, fearful and trembling. She fell before him and told everyone what had just happened. Her fear was unfounded. Jesus said to her, "Daughter, your faith has made you well; go in peace" (Lk 8:48). In this brief encounter Jesus revealed his knowledge of this woman's need, healed her, comforted her, brought her from the darkness of shame to the light of dignity, and encouraged the faith of others. Jesus was concerned about her in all her uniqueness and complexity. Such is his concern for each of us. Through the sacraments Jesus continues today to free us from fear, to heal us, to comfort us, to restore our dignity, and to strengthen the faith of others through us.

From the Gospels to the Mass

The power that came forth from Jesus during his earthly ministry continues to come forth today. The *Catechism of the Catholic Church* cites this Gospel passage of the woman's healing to explain how Jesus acts now in the sacraments: "The sick try to touch him, 'for power came forth from him and healed them all.' And so in the sacraments Christ continues to 'touch' us in order to heal us" (CCC 1504). In the words of Saint Leo the Great (†461), "what was visible in our Savior has passed over into his mysteries [sacraments]."[22]

During Jesus' earthly ministry, glimpses of his power and glory, such as the miraculous catch of fish and the transfiguration, terrified his disciples. Now in the sacraments God accommodates his presence and actions to our frail nature. Christ, with the Father and the Holy Spirit, acts in the sacraments through signs and symbols such as water, oil, bread, and wine, through words and songs, through postures and gestures, through candles and incense, through color and images. By the powerful working of the Holy Spirit these liturgical signs "become bearers of the saving and sanctifying action of Christ" (CCC 1189). In this way Jesus continues to do among us today all that he did during his earthly ministry. His action in the Eucharist—the Sacrament of sacraments, the Great Sacrament—is preeminent (see CCC 1169). All of the other sacraments and ministries of the Church draw from and are directed toward the Eucharist, because "in the most Blessed Eucharist is contained the whole spiritual good of the Church, namely Christ himself."[23]

The Work of the Trinity

In their commentary on the healing of the woman with the hemorrhages, some Church Fathers emphasized that this healing was the work of the Trinity—Father, Son, and Holy Spirit. Saint Ephrem the Syrian (†373), for example, noted the joint work of Jesus and his Father, "Because his [the Father's] power had become resplendent, and had magnified the Son."[24] Saint Hilary (†368) wrote that this miracle was the joint work of the Son and the Holy Spirit, who descended on Jesus at his Baptism: "She with the apostles reached out for the gift of the Holy Spirit from the body of Christ in the form of a garment's hem as he walked by, and she is immediately healed."[25] We can say, then, that Jesus' miracles are manifestations of the Father's power radiant in the Son and going forth in the Holy Spirit.

In their references to the work of the Father, the Son, and the Holy Spirit, the Church Fathers teach us an important truth about the Trinity: God's work in the world is accomplished by the joint working of the three Persons of the Trinity. The Son is conceived in the womb of the Blessed Virgin Mary when the Holy Spirit comes upon her, and the power of the Most High, the Father, overshadows her (see Lk 1:35). When Jesus is baptized, the Spirit descends upon him and the voice of the Father is heard from heaven saying, "You are my Son, the Beloved; with you I am well pleased" (Lk 3:22). On the cross Jesus "in freedom and love offered his life to his Father through the Holy Spirit in reparation for our disobedience" (CCC 614). Even in the resurrection "the three divine persons act together as one" (CCC 648).

Although everything that God does in the world is the work of the Trinity, each Person works "according to his unique personal property" (CCC 258). In other words, different activities are assigned to different Persons. In theological language this is called appropriation; that is, a given activity is *appropriated* to a specific divine Person. Saint Paul's blessing at the end of Second Corinthians is a good example: "The grace of the Lord Jesus Christ, the love of God, and the communion of the Holy Spirit be with all of you" (13:13). Grace, love, and communion are the common work of the Trinity, but Saint Paul appropriates each to a particular Person.

The Trinity "is the central mystery of Christian faith and life. It is the mystery of God in himself" (CCC 234). The liturgy offers us a starting point for understanding the Trinitarian mystery. Eucharistic Prayer IV gives a summary of the mission—the unique personal property—of each Person of the Trinity. The prayer begins by addressing God the Father: You, Father, have "made all that is, so that you might fill your creatures with blessings and bring joy to many of them by the glory of your light."[26] The mission of the Son is to proclaim "to the poor . . . the good news of salvation, to prisoners, freedom, and to the sorrowful of heart, joy."[27] The mission of the Holy Spirit is to bring "to perfection his [the Father's] work in the world," to "sanctify creation to the full," and to enable us to "live no longer for ourselves but for him who died and rose again for us."[28] Thus, in every celebration of the Eucharist God the Father blesses us and brings us joy, God the Son proclaims good news to the poor, freedom to those imprisoned both outwardly and inwardly, and joy to the sorrowing, and God the Holy Spirit is perfecting the Father's work in creation and enabling us to live for Christ.

Increase Our Faith

When Jesus healed the woman suffering from a twelve-year illness, he emphasized the importance of faith when he told her, "Your faith has made you well" (Mt 9:22). Faith was a prominent factor in many of Jesus' miracles. When the friends of a paralytic lowered him through the roof, "Jesus saw their faith" and proceeded to heal the man and forgive him of his sins (Mk 2:1–12). When he encountered the two blind men crying out, "Have mercy on us, Son of David!" he asked them, "Do you believe that I am able to do this?" (Mt 9:27, 28). He encouraged "filial boldness" when he told his disciples, "Whatever you ask for in prayer, believe that you have received it, and it will be yours" (Mk 11:24). In his encounter with the father of the boy possessed by a mute spirit (see Mk 9:14–29), Jesus affirmed the importance of faith. The disciples had tried and failed to cast out the spirit, and in desperation the boy's father said to Jesus, "If you are able to do anything, have pity on us and help us" (v. 22). Jesus replied, "All things can be done for the one who believes" (v. 23). Finally, when he encountered the Roman centurion (see Mt 8:5–10) and the Canaanite woman (see Mt 15:22–28), he commended their great faith and granted their requests.

While Jesus praised great faith, he also lamented the little-ness or lack of faith. To those who doubted that God would provide for their needs, he pointed to the beauty of the flowers of the field and asked, "Will he not much more clothe you— you of little faith?" (Mt 6:30). To his terrified disciples who woke him when a storm arose while they were crossing the sea, Jesus asked, "Why are you afraid, you of little faith?" (Mt 8:26). To Peter who had started to sink as he was walking on the water toward Jesus, he said, "You of little faith, why did you doubt?" (Mt 14:31). A lack of faith even affected Jesus' ability to perform miracles. When he returned to his hometown and his neighbors took offense at him, "he did not do many deeds of power there, because of their unbelief" (Mt 13:58).

These examples illustrate the essential role of faith in the Christian life and invite us to look more closely at our own faith. What is faith? *Faith is our personal response to an encounter with God who reveals himself freely to us.* Our faith is in a person, not in propositions. To say that I have faith in God means that "I entrust myself freely to a God who is Father and who loves me; it is adherence to a 'You' who gives me hope and trust."[29] To believe in Jesus is to "personally welcome him into our lives and journey toward him, clinging to him in love and following in his footsteps along the way" (LF 18). Furthermore, the confession "I believe in you" has two aspects—I believe in God, *and* I believe in the truth that he has revealed about himself, about me, and about the world. The Christian confession "I believe" refers to my belief in God and to what he teaches because I trust him.

Faith includes not only our belief in the Trinity and in the truth revealed to us by God the Father, Christ his Word, and the Spirit of truth, but also our active trust. Jesus' responses to those of little faith reveal that people bear some responsibility for the level of their faith. At the same time, Peter's confession that Jesus is the Messiah (see Mt 16:16) illustrates that faith is also a gift from God. When Peter confessed that Jesus was the Christ, the Son of God, Jesus told him that his confession came, not from himself, but from the Father. There are, then, two dimensions to faith: it is a virtue gifted to us by God, and it is something that God asks us to nourish and exercise.

How can we nourish and strengthen our faith? The *Catechism* suggests three ways: "To live, grow, and persevere in the faith until the end we must nourish it with the word of God; we must beg the Lord to increase our faith; it must be 'working through charity,' abounding in hope, and rooted in the faith of the Church" (CCC 162).

First, we can strengthen our faith by reading and meditating on the word of God. As Saint Jerome famously taught, "Ignorance of the Scriptures is ignorance of Christ."[30] When we read the Sacred Scriptures, we come to know Christ and what he has revealed to us. The Old Testament recounts God's preparation for the coming of Christ. It is "a store of sublime teaching about God, sound wisdom about human life, and a wonderful treasury of prayers, and in them, the mystery of our salvation is present in a hidden way."[31] The books of the New Testament "hand on the ultimate truth of God's Revelation. Their central object is Jesus Christ, God's incarnate Son: his acts, teachings, Passion and glorification, and his Church's beginnings under the Spirit's guidance" (CCC 124).

God's definitive revelation in Christ provides the key to understanding the Old Testament through a method called typology. Typology interprets Old Testament persons (e.g., Isaac, Moses, and David), events (e.g., Israel's exodus from Egypt), or things (e.g., sacrifices, manna, the bronze serpent) as "types" (or prototypes) of what God definitively fulfilled in the person of Christ. Baptism, for example, was prefigured by the flood and Israel's miraculous escape through the Red Sea, and the gift of manna prefigured Christ and the Eucharist. Typology is often used to explain aspects of the Eucharist, and we will encounter it throughout this book, especially in the teaching of Saint John Chrysostom in Chapter 8. An old saying summarizes the relationship between the two testaments: "The New Testament lies hidden in the Old and the Old Testament is unveiled in the New" (CCC 129).

The second way the *Catechism* encourages us to increase our faith is to "beg the Lord to increase our faith" (CCC 162) to know him better, to understand his teaching more deeply, and to trust him more. An incident from the Gospels illustrates this well: Jesus' encounter with the boy possessed by a mute spirit (see Mk 9:14–29). The father questioned Jesus' power to help his son, to which Jesus replied, "All things can be done for the one who believes" (Mk 9:22–23). With humility and honesty the father replied, "I believe; help my unbelief!" (Mk 9:24). "Behold faith," wrote Saint Augustine, "yet not full faith. . . . 'I believe': therefore there was faith; but 'help my unbelief': therefore there was not full faith."[32] We see the same desire in the apostles' request to Jesus, "Increase our faith" (Lk 17:5). Theirs too was an incomplete faith, wrote Saint Augustine, for they would not have made this request "if they had full faith."[33] Our faith is also maturing, and in times of difficulty and doubt these prayers can also be our prayers: Increase my faith. I do believe; help my unbelief.

Third, the *Catechism* teaches that a growing faith is marked by charity, hope, and union with the Church. Saint Paul gave the Thessalonians—and us—a concise summary of charity in action, exhorting them to "admonish the idlers, encourage the fainthearted, help the weak, be patient with all of them" (1 Thess 5:14). Faith is also nourished by hope. Christian hope is rooted in the person of Christ and in the assurance "when he is revealed, we will be like him, for we will see him as he is" (1 Jn 3:2). Scripture promises us, "All who have this hope in him purify themselves, just as he is pure" (1 Jn 3:3). In addition, a growing faith must be formed by the faith of the Church. This begins at Baptism, which unites us to Christ and to his Body, the Church. The Church in turn hands on to her members what she has received from Christ, "the new light born of an encounter with the true God, a light which touches us at the core of our being and engages our minds, wills, and emotions, opening us to relationships lived in communion" (LF 40).

At each Mass we can place our faith—weak and wavering though it may be—on the altar as our offering to God, to be strengthened, renewed, and transformed by his Spirit. At each Mass we can bring our faith to the table of his banquet, to be nourished and strengthened by the Body and Blood of Christ.

Love Itself Is Knowing

Saint Anselm (†1109) stated another essential aspect of faith: "Faith *seeks understanding*."[34] Our model and our intercessor for this is the Blessed Virgin Mary, who treasured up and pondered on the events of Christ's conception and birth (see Lk 2:19). Our faith grows stronger as we deepen our understanding of the One in whom we have placed our faith, for the lover wants to know the beloved better, and "a more penetrating knowledge will in turn call forth a greater faith, increasingly set afire by love" (CCC 158). As this indicates, faith and love are intertwined, for love itself is a kind of knowing.

Saint Gregory the Great (†604), in a commentary on John 15:16, wrote, "When we love the supercelestial things we have heard about, we already know the things we love, because *love itself is knowledge*."[35] While knowledge deepens our love, love itself is one of the ways that we know God. William of Saint-Thierry (†1147/8), a Cistercian monk and close friend of Saint Bernard of Clairvaux (†1153), was particularly taken with Saint Gregory's insight. In a catechesis on

William of Saint-Thierry, Pope Benedict XVI discussed William's development of this theme. According to the Pope, William said that love transforms and unites the lover and the beloved, permitting "a far deeper knowledge than that which is brought by reason alone. A famous saying of William expresses it: '*Amor ipse intellectus est*—love in itself is already the beginning of knowledge.'" Our own experience, continues the Pope, confirms the truth of this saying.

> Dear friends, let us ask ourselves: is not our life just like this? Is it not perhaps true that we only truly know *who* and *what* we love? Without a certain fondness one knows no one and nothing! And this applies first of all to the knowledge of God and his mysteries that exceed our mental capacity to understand: God is known if he is loved![36]

Faith and love are both essential for a fruitful reception of the Body and Blood of Christ. Saint Teresa of Avila understood their intrinsic connection. "Certainly, I think that if we were to approach the most Blessed Sacrament with great faith and love, once would be enough to leave us rich." She recognized, however, two obstacles to receiving Communion with great faith and love. The first is routine. "The trouble," she wrote, is that we receive Communion "out of routine and it shows." The second is the world. "O miserable world," she lamented, "you have so covered the eyes of those who live in you that they do not see the treasures by which they could win everlasting riches!"[37] But she never doubted the Lord's goodness and generosity: "Oh, God help me; and how he strengthens faith and increases love!"[38]

Nurturing Eucharistic Amazement

This chapter has explored how the power that came forth from Jesus during his earthly ministry continues to come forth in the Eucharist.

- ✦ Jesus praised great faith. The prayers for faith of the disciples and the desperate father—"Lord, increase my faith" and "I do believe, help my unbelief"—are powerful prayers you can make your own. You could pray one before Mass begins and the other as you approach the altar for Communion.

- ✦ Saint Jerome insisted on the importance of nourishing our faith by meditating on Sacred Scripture. Read the Sunday readings during the week, or read and reflect on the Creed that is recited at Mass.

- ✦ Finally, faith and love are intertwined, and love itself is a way of knowing. You could ask yourself the following questions: What do I love about Jesus, not just know, but *love*? What events in the Gospel do I have a special affection for? Writing a personal litany is a way to increase your love for Jesus:

  Jesus, you are gentle and humble, I love you.
  Jesus, you comforted the widow of Nain, I love you.
  Jesus, you _____, I love you.

These are ways to nourish both knowledge and one's personal relationship with the Lord.

———————————•———————————

Conclusion

The power of Jesus' earthly ministry evoked astonishment and even fear. Yet his power is not a thing of the past. The power of Jesus remains present in his Body, the Church, and continues "to go forth" in a special way through the sacraments, particularly the Eucharist. This power is the joint working of the Father, the Son, and the Holy Spirit. In the next chapter we will learn from a saint who believed in, experienced, and taught these truths—Saint Teresa of Avila.

NOTES

21. This account is recorded in Mt 9:20–22; Mk 5:25–34; and Lk 8:43–48.

22. *Catechism of the Catholic Church*, 1115 [St. Leo the Great, *Sermo.* 74, 2: PL 54, 398].

23. Vatican Council II, *Presbyterorum Ordinis* (December 7, 1965), The Holy See, Vatican.va, 5. https://www.vatican.va/archive/hist_councils/ii_vatican_council/documents/vat-ii_decree_ 19651207_presbyterorum-ordinis_en.html.

24. Ephrem, *Saint Ephrem's Commentary on Tatians's Diatessaron: An English Translation of* Chester Beatty *Syriac MS 709 with Introduction and Notes* (Oxford University Press, 1993), 129.

25. Hilary of Poitiers, *Commentary on Matthew*, trans. D.H. Williams, *The Fathers of the Church, Vol. 125* (Washington, DC: Catholic University of America Press, 2012), 106.

26. *The Roman Missal*, English translation according to the Third Typical Edition (Totowa, NJ: Catholic Book Publishing, 2011), (EP IV) 116.

27. *Roman Missal*, Order of Mass 117.

28. *Roman Missal*, Order of Mass 117.

29. Benedict XVI, "General Audience, The Year of Faith: What is faith?" October 24, 2012, The Holy See, Vatican.va. https://www.vatican.va/content/benedict-xvi/en/audiences/2012/documents/hf_ben-xvi_aud_20121024.html.

30. Vatican Council II, *Dei Verbum* (November 18, 1965), The Holy See, Vatican.va, 25. https://www.vatican.va/archive/hist_councils/ii_vatican_council/documents/vat-ii_const_19651118_dei-verbum_en.html.

31. Vatican Council II, *Dei Verbum*, 15.

32. Augustine, *Sermon on the Mount; Harmony of the Gospels; Homilies on the Gospels*, trans. Philip Schaff, NPNF 6, 65.1.454.

33. Augustine, *Sermon on the Mount*, NPNF 6, 65.1.454.

34. *Catechism of the Catholic Church*, 158 [St. Anselm, *Prosl. Prooem.*: PL 153, 225A].

35. Gregory the Great, *Forty Gospel Homilies*, trans. Dom David Hurst (Kalamazoo: Cistercian Publications, 1990), 215. Italics added.

36. Benedict XVI, "General Audience, William of Saint-Thierry," December 2, 2009, The Holy See. Vatican.va. https://www.vatican.va/content/benedict-xvi/en/audiences/2009/documents/hf_ben-xvi_aud_20091202.html.

37. Teresa of Avila, *The Collected Works of St. Teresa of Avila, Volume Two*, trans. Kieran Kavanaugh and Otilio Rodriguez (Washington, DC: ICS Publications, 1980), 241.

38. Teresa of Avila, *The Collected Works of St. Teresa of Avila, Volume One*, trans. Kieran Kavanaugh and Otilio Rodriguez (Washington, DC: ICS Publications, 1980), 221.

Chapter 3

Christ Himself Is Present:
Saint Teresa of Avila

Behold him here . . . full of glory . . . strengthening some, encouraging others, our companion in the most Blessed Sacrament; it doesn't seem it was in his power to leave us for even a moment.

SAINT TERESA OF AVILA, *THE BOOK OF HER LIFE*

IN THE EUCHARIST CHRIST is truly, substantially, and personally present, and all that he did during his earthly ministry he now continues to do in the sacraments, preeminently in the Eucharist. Saint Teresa of Avila ardently believed this mystery. "Now, then," she wrote in *The Way of Perfection*, "if when he went about in the world the mere touch of his robes cured the sick, why doubt, if we have faith, that miracles will be worked while he is within us and that he will give what we ask of him, since he is in our house?" As this quote reveals, Teresa knew that Christ was fully present in the Eucharist and able to perform today the same miracles that he worked during his earthly ministry. She also understood the importance of our faith in Christ's Eucharistic presence as well as the possibility of doubt. Most importantly, she was convinced of the goodness and generosity of God when Christ is received with great faith and love. Teresa wryly observed, "His Majesty is not accustomed to paying poorly for his lodging if the hospitality is good."[39]

Her Life

Saint Teresa of Avila was born in Avila, Spain on March 28, 1515, the third of nine children. At the age of twenty she entered the Carmelite Convent of the Incarnation at Avila. For many years her prayer and devotion were mixed with what she called vanities, but in 1554 at the age of thirty-nine, while praying before a statue of Christ, she experienced a powerful conversion and began to pursue spiritual perfection. Within a few years, the Lord led her to reform the Carmelite Order and to reinstitute the strict observance of the primitive Carmelite rule. Despite much suspicion and opposition, she founded the first convent of the Discalced Reform, Saint Joseph's in Avila, in 1562. This would be the first of seventeen Carmels (monasteries) of women she founded during the last twenty years of her life. In 1567 she met Saint John of the Cross (†1591) and persuaded the young Carmelite monk to join her work, a collaboration and friendship that profoundly influenced their lives, the Carmelite Order, and Catholic spirituality. In 1572 after receiving Communion from Saint John of the Cross she experienced the spiritual marriage, in which she saw the Lord give his right hand to her and say, "Behold this nail; it is a sign you will be my bride from today on."[40] She died in 1582. Her major writings are *The Story of Her Life*; *The Way of Perfection*, a commentary on the Lord's Prayer; *The Book of Her Foundations*, an account of the convents she founded; and her masterpiece, *The Interior Castle*. In addition, she wrote several smaller works, including spiritual testimonies, descriptions of her spiritual experiences recorded in a sort of spiritual journal, meditations on the Song of Songs, and poetry. She was canonized in 1622 and declared a Doctor of the Church by Saint Paul VI in 1970, the first woman saint to receive this title. Her feast day is October 15.

In this chapter we will study Teresa's descriptions of her own Eucharistic experiences. Saint Teresa received many extraordinary graces during Mass that most Catholics may never experience. By presenting them I do not mean to suggest we should be seeking these experiences. Instead, I believe Saint Teresa's experiences can increase our own faith in the power of the Eucharist. Saint John of the Cross' wise and enduring advice is pertinent here. Christians should not, he wrote, be "trying to get some feeling and satisfaction rather than humbly praising and reverencing God dwelling within them." These spiritual experiences are beautiful blessings bestowed by Christ in the Eucharist, but "the invisible grace it gives is a greater blessing," and we should "set the eyes of faith on this invisible grace."[41]

A Vision of Glory

Teresa's understanding of the Eucharist was profoundly influenced by a vision she received of Christ's glory. In *The Story of Her Life*, Teresa described this vision:

> I saw the most sacred humanity with more extraordinary glory than I had ever seen. It was made manifest to me through a knowledge admirable and clear that the humanity was taken into the bosom of the Father. I wouldn't know how to describe the nature of this, because, without my seeing anything, it seemed to me I was in the presence of the Divinity.

Teresa saw this vision four times, and it transformed her understanding of Communion.

> When I approached to receive Communion and recalled that extraordinary majesty I had seen and considered that it was present in the Blessed Sacrament (the Lord often desires that I behold it in the Host), my hair stood on end; the whole experience seemed to annihilate me.

The contrast between the humble outward appearance of bread and the Person it concealed astonished Teresa:

> When I behold majesty as extraordinary as this concealed in something as small as the Host, it happens afterward that I marvel at wisdom so wonderful, and I fail to know how the Lord gives me the courage or strength to approach him.

Just the remembrance of this vision moved Teresa to prayer:

May the angels and all creatures praise you, for you so mea-sure things in accordance with our weakness that when we rejoice in your sovereign favors your great power does not so frighten us that, as weak and wretched people, we would not dare enjoy them.[42]

In this prayer Teresa expressed her amazement at the majesty of God concealed beneath the humble appearances of bread and wine, the way that God accommodates himself in the Eucharist to our weakness, and the power that God communicates to us through the sacrament.

A Great Medicine

Throughout her life Teresa suffered from poor health. The year after she made her profession of vows she became gravely ill, and the doctors were unable to find a cure. Her father took her to a well-known quack whose treatments almost killed her. She eventually recovered through the intercession of Saint Joseph, but most likely due to these harsh treatments she struggled with poor health and numerous illnesses all her life. A doctor who examined her toward the end of her life stated that it was difficult to isolate her main problem because she was afflicted by so many ailments.

The Eucharist often brought Teresa relief from her ill-nesses. In an account of her soul to her spiritual director she wrote, "I have experienced for more than a half year that at least when I am receiving Communion I noticeably and clearly feel bodily health."[43] She also shared this experience with her nuns in *The Way of Perfection*:

Do you think this heavenly food fails to provide sustenance, even for these bodies, that it is not a great medicine even for bodily ills? I know that it is. I know a person with serious illnesses, who often experiences great pain, who through this bread had them taken away as though by a gesture of the hand and was made completely well.[44]

The person Teresa is describing here is herself.

In addition to physical healing, the Eucharist brought Teresa other kinds of relief and comfort. For example, she described experiences of profound peace at the time of Communion. Often she would feel this peace as she was preparing to receive the Lord: "In approaching to receive Communion, my soul and body will become very quiet, and my intellect very sound and clear, and I will feel all the fortitude and desires I usually have."[45] Other times this sense of peace came after she had received Communion. On many occasions the Eucharist also brought her relief from suffering, fatigue, and confusion.

And sometimes in approaching the Sacrament I felt at once so good in soul and body that I was surprised. It seems that in only a moment all the darknesses of the soul disperse; and once the sun is out, the soul recognizes the foolishness in which it was held.

The Lord also brought Teresa comfort by a word after Communion. "Only by his saying, 'Don't grow weary, don't be afraid,' as I've already mentioned elsewhere, I was left completely cured; or by seeing some vision, as though I had not suffered anything."[46] In the Eucharist Christ brought Teresa healing, light, and peace.

Nurturing Eucharistic Amazement

Saint Teresa is a powerful witness that Jesus cares about and responds to our personal needs and concerns during Mass.

- When you are experiencing physical or emotional problems, turn to the Lord and ask him to heal you.

- The Mass includes the promise and blessing of God's peace following the Our Father. At this point you can add your own personal petitions.

- You can also bring the needs of others to Christ, just as the paralytic's friends brought him to Jesus (see Mk 2:3–12). For example, you could pray for healing for those who have been abused by priests and for comfort and blessing for those who feel that no one cares for them (see Ps 142:4).

He Provides the Counsel

Through the Eucharist the Lord also guided and encouraged Teresa in her work of reforming the Carmelite Order. For example, she described how the Lord encouraged her while she was in the process of establishing her first convent, Saint Joseph in Avila. "One day after Communion, his Majesty earnestly commanded me to strive for this new monastery with all my powers, and he made great promises that it would be founded and that he would be highly served in it."[47] Teresa was greatly reassured by these words for she knew well the power of the Lord's promises.

A year before making her first foundation, she received important encouragement for her reform work on August 12, 1561, the feast day of Saint Clare (†1253), a friend and disciple of Saint Francis of Assisi. Teresa described her experience:

> While I was going to Communion, Saint Clare appeared to me with striking beauty. She told me to take courage and to continue on with what I had begun, that she would help me. I became very devoted to her; and what she said has indeed come true.[48]

It is significant that as Saint Teresa was beginning her reform work she received a visit from Saint Clare, one of the great Catholic reformers. She was "the first woman to write her own rule for her community," demonstrating "that women could govern themselves in community."[49] Teresa would follow in Saint Clare's footsteps and write a new rule for her Carmelite houses.

On February 9, 1570, the Lord encouraged Teresa after Communion to persevere in her reform. In this vision she saw Christ wearing a radiant crown over the wounds made by the crown of thorns. Jesus told her that she should grieve over the many wounds he was now receiving. Deeply moved by this vision, Teresa asked the Lord what she could do. He urged her to press ahead with the foundation of new monasteries and told her that she should write an account of their foundation. Teresa completed *The Book of Her Foundations*, her fourth and final book, in 1582, the year she died.

Teresa also received guidance and encouragement for others during Mass. A rector Teresa knew "was very persecuted and found himself in deep affliction." Teresa described how she received words of encouragement for him.

> One day, while I was hearing Mass, at the elevation of the host, I saw Christ on the cross. He spoke some words of consolation that I was to tell this rector and some other words foretelling what was to come and reminding the rector of what Christ suffered for him and announcing that he should prepare himself to suffer.

Teresa did as the Lord directed her, and it "gave the rector great consolation and courage, and everything came about afterward as the Lord had told me."[50]

Teresa believed that the Lord also guided and instructed others through the Eucharist. For several years her confessor was a young Jesuit priest, Father Baltasar Alvarez. He was only twenty-five or twenty-six when he began to direct Teresa, and the first years were particularly difficult for him. He had to reply to those who were skeptical of Teresa's extraordinary experiences, calm Teresa's fears about being misled, and reassure her about the visions she received. "Since in each vision there was something new," she wrote, "God permitted that I afterward be left with great fears." Father Alvarez successfully met each of these challenges, and Teresa believed that his insight and counsel came from the Eucharist: "God gave him understanding of the truth in all things—the very Sacrament itself enlightened him, I believe."[51] Teresa could only marvel at the Lord's goodness, power, and love: "Oh, what a good God! Oh, how good a Lord and how powerful! He provides not only the counsel but also the remedy! His words are works!"[52]

Nurturing Eucharistic Amazement

Teresa received from Jesus in the Eucharist consolation and courage, guidance and light, both for herself and for others.

- ✦ Take advantage of the periods of silence during the Liturgy of the Word so that the Holy Spirit can apply to you personally and specifically the word that has been proclaimed.

- ✦ Like Teresa, ask for direction and enlightenment during the Communion Rite, both as you are coming to the altar to receive the Eucharistic Lord and after you have received him.

Deep Interior Secrets Revealed

In addition to guidance on practical matters and difficult situations, Teresa received through the Eucharist a deeper knowledge of the truths of the Catholic faith. Teresa had a great and sustained interest in the Trinity. On one occasion she wondered if the three Persons always worked together. "Could the Son create an ant without the Father?" she asked. "No, for it is all one power, and the same goes for the Holy Spirit; thus there is only one all-powerful God and all three Persons are one Majesty."[53] In 1572 she "reflected that only the Son took human flesh,"[54] but it was only three years later that the Lord gave her the understanding of "how the Person of the Son, and not the others, took flesh." Unfortunately for us, she then wrote, "I wouldn't know how to explain any of these things."[55] We can only wish that she had tried!

Teresa wanted to understand how the Trinity is one God in three Persons, admitting in 1572 that she used to think of the three Persons as "three faces . . . painted on one body."[56] This desire may partially explain an experience she had on the feast of Saint Augustine on August 28, 1575. She wrote that on this day after Communion "I understood—I'm unable to say how—and almost saw (although it was something intellectual and passed quickly) how the three Persons of the Blessed Trinity, which I bear imprinted in my soul, are one."[57] That Teresa received this insight into the mystery of the Trinity on the feast of Saint Augustine is noteworthy because Saint Augustine wrote one of the most important and profound works on Trinitarian theology—*On the Trinity*. Although Saint Augustine wrote most of his books at the request of others or in response to a theological controversy, he wrote *On the Trinity* for himself, "to contemplate the Trinity within the human soul."[58] It is an example of faith seeking understanding that illustrates the close connection between theology and spirituality. During the Mass on his feast day over 1100 years later, the Lord gave Teresa a new understanding of the unity of the Trinity.[59] Later that year Teresa observed that "there are deep interior secrets revealed when one receives Communion."[60]

Be With Him Willingly

Considering how frequently the graces Teresa received came during or after Communion, it is not surprising that she placed special emphasis on spending time with the Lord following Communion. In her commentary on the Lord's Prayer, she described her practice at Communion. She knew the importance of faith, so she "strove to strengthen her faith so that in receiving her Lord it was as if, with her bodily eyes, she saw him enter her house." When "this Lord truly entered her poor home," she made every effort to set aside every distraction and "freed herself from all exterior things when it was possible and entered to be with him." She focused all her thoughts and her senses on him "so that all of them would take notice of so great a good . . . [and] would not impede the soul from recognizing it." Even though she didn't necessarily experience any consolations or "feel devotion, faith told her that he was indeed there."

Teresa advised her nuns to adopt the same practice. "Be with him willingly," she told them. "Don't lose so good an occasion for conversing with him as is the hour after having received Communion . . . since you have the Person himself present." Drawing on passages from the Gospels—Mary sitting at the feet of Jesus (see Lk 10:39) and the sinful woman who sought him in the home of the Pharisee (see Lk 7:38) —she exhorted her sisters, "This, then, is a good time for our Master to teach us, and for us to listen to him, kiss his feet because he wanted to teach us, and beg him not to leave."

Teresa also advised her nuns about distractions and wandering thoughts after Communion. "If you immediately turn your thoughts to other things, if you pay no attention and take no account of the fact that he is within you, how will he be able to reveal himself to you?" When this happens, she asks, "What is there for him to do? Must he force us to see him, since he wants to reveal himself to us?" Those who receive Communion and then immediately turn their attention elsewhere are like those who during his earthly life "didn't treat him so well when he let himself be seen openly by all and told them clearly who he was; very few were those who believed him."[61] Immediately following Communion, she insisted, "There's no reason to go looking for him in some other place farther away."[62]

Teresa also knew that the enemy would often try to hinder one's recollection after Communion.

> Now then, Sisters, consider that if in the beginning you do not fare well (for it could be that the devil will make you feel afflicted and constrained in heart since he knows the

great damage that will be caused him by this recollection), the devil will make you think you find more devotion in other things and less in this recollection after Communion. Do not abandon this practice; the Lord will see in it how much you love him.[63]

Teresa had no illusions about the subtlety and variety of the enemy's attacks: affliction, interior resistance, even temptations to seek spiritual consolation elsewhere when we have the Lord within us. The key is to always remember the one important thing: "Receiving Communion is not like picturing with the imagination. . . . In Communion the event is happening now, and it is entirely true."[64]

Desire Him Greatly

Teresa emphasized the importance of our desire for the Lord and our longing to receive him in the Eucharist. "He doesn't want to show himself openly, communicate his grandeurs, and give his treasures," she said, "except to those who he knows desire him greatly; these are his true friends." And to his true friends he is immensely generous: "So his Majesty is being merciful enough to all of us who love him, by letting us know that it is he who is present in the most Blessed Sacrament."[65]

It is our desire that enables us to perceive him under the appearances of bread and wine.

Though he comes disguised, the disguise as I have said, does not prevent him from being recognized in many ways, in conformity with the desire we have to see him. And you can desire to see him so much that he will reveal himself to you entirely.[66]

In the words of her great friend and collaborator, Saint John of the Cross, "Love is paid only with love itself."[67]

Receive Him Worthily

The Apostle Paul warned the Corinthians concerning the worthy reception of the Eucharist:

> Whoever, therefore, eats the bread or drinks the cup of the Lord in an unworthy manner will be answerable for the body and blood of the Lord. Examine yourselves, and only then eat of the bread and drink of the cup. For all who eat and drink without discerning the body, eat and drink judgment against themselves. (1 Cor 11:27–29)

The importance of Saint Paul's admonition was brought home to Teresa in a vision she received of a priest in mortal sin.

> Once, while approaching to receive Communion, I saw with my soul's eyes more clearly than with my bodily eyes two devils whose appearance was abominable. It seems to me their horns were wrapped around the poor priest's throat, and in the host that was going to be given to me I saw my Lord with the majesty I mentioned placed in the priest's hands, which were clearly seen to be his offender's; and I understood that that soul was in mortal sin.

Through this vision the Lord taught Teresa three things: first, how important it is for priests to be holy; second, how terrible it is to receive the Eucharist unworthily; and third, the devil's power over someone in mortal sin. This vision, terrifying in its power, deepened Teresa's zeal for holiness and her reverence for the Eucharist: "It did me a great deal of good and brought me deep understanding of what I owed God. May he be blessed forever and ever."[68]

Conclusion

The Lord gave Saint Teresa of Avila extraordinary experiences and profound insights about the Eucharist to share with the Church. Her vision of Christ in glory reminds us of the grandeur hidden beneath the appearances of bread and wine. The relief she received from physical suffering and emotional trials increases our faith. The guidance that she received for herself and others from the Eucharist encourages us to ask for the same. The insights she received into the mysteries of the faith encourage us to know better the One who gives himself completely to us. The visions and understanding she received about spending time with Christ after Communion, strengthening her desire for him, and receiving him worthily are powerful incentives to our own growth in holiness. She knew that what she had been given was meant for others, and she shared her Eucharistic amazement with fervor and urgency.

Notes

39. Teresa of Avila, *Collected Works*, 2:172.
40. Teresa of Avila, *Collected Works*, 1:402.

41. John of the Cross, *Collected Works of St. John of the Cross*, trans. Kieran Kavanaugh and Otilio Rodriguez (Washington, DC: ICS Publications, 1991), 372.

42. Teresa of Avila, *Collected Works*, 1:336–37.

43. Teresa of Avila, *Collected Works*, 1:378.

44. Teresa of Avila, *Collected Works*, 2:171.

45. Teresa of Avila, *Collected Works*, 1:378.

46. Teresa of Avila, *Collected Works*, 1:260.

47. Teresa of Avila, *Collected Works*, 1:280.

48. Teresa of Avila, *Collected Works*, 1:290.

49. C. Colt Anderson, *The Great Catholic Reformers: From Gregory the Great to Dorothy Day* (New York: Paulist Press, 2007), 81.

50. Teresa of Avila, *Collected Works*, 1:335.

51. Teresa of Avila, *Collected Works*, 1:245.

52. Teresa of Avila, *Collected Works*, 1:221.

53. Teresa of Avila, *Collected Works*, 1:401.

54. Teresa of Avila, *Collected Works*, 1:400.

55. Teresa of Avila, *Collected Works*, 1:414.

56. Teresa of Avila, *Collected Works*, 1:400.

57. Teresa of Avila, *Collected Works*, 1:410.

58. Augustine, *Augustine of Hippo: Selected Writings*, 17.

59. See Teresa of Avila, *Collected Works*, 1:410.

60. Teresa of Avila, *Collected Works*, 1:415.

61. Teresa of Avila, *Collected Works*, 2:171–74.

62. Teresa of Avila, *Collected Works*, 2:172.

63. Teresa of Avila, *Collected Works*, 2:175.

64. Teresa of Avila, *Collected Works*, 2:172.

65. Teresa of Avila, *Collected Works*, 2:174.

66. Teresa of Avila, *Collected Works*, 2:173.

67. John of the Cross, *Collected Works of St. John of the Cross*, 506. Saint Thérèse of Lisieux quotes this saying in her Autobiography.

68. Teresa of Avila, *Collected Works*, 1:338–39.

CHAPTER 4

The Mass:
The Renewal of the Covenant

The Covenant is a relationship: God's gift of himself to
man, but also man's response to God.

CARDINAL RATZINGER,
THE SPIRIT OF THE LITURGY

WE HAVE EXPLORED HOW Saint Teresa of Avila
described the graces she received during Mass and
considered ways in which her experiences could be applied to
our own participation in the Mass. While each person receives
specific graces from God in this sacramental encounter, the
Mass has a larger purpose—the renewal of his Covenant with
his children. When Jesus instituted the Eucharist at the Last
Supper, he spoke of the New Covenant as he gave the chalice
to his disciples, "This cup is the new covenant in my blood,"

and he commanded them to celebrate it until his return: "Do this, as often as you drink it, in remembrance of me" (1 Cor 11:25). Every celebration of the Mass renews the New Covenant that Christ instituted at the Last Supper and "draws the faithful into the compelling love of Christ and sets them on fire" (SC 10).

We turn our attention now to reflect on the Mass as a renewal of the New Covenant. After a brief look at the history and theology of the Covenant, we will walk through the Mass, discovering how the Covenant is renewed through the different parts of the Mass. We will begin by asking three questions: What is a covenant? How did Old Testament covenants prefigure the New Covenant? How is the Covenant renewed in the Mass?

What Is a Covenant?

Pope Benedict XVI, writing as Cardinal Ratzinger, explained the centrality of the Covenant. "The goal of creation," he wrote, "is the Covenant, the love story of God and man."[69] In the ancient Near East culture of the Old Testament, covenants included different types of agreements and contracts, including friendships and marriages, and we find examples of these in the Bible. Unique to the Bible, however, was the revelation of a covenant between humans and God. God's covenants with individuals (e.g., Noah, Abraham) and with Israel were not agreements between equals, "but a pure gift of God. By this gift of his love God bridges every distance and truly makes us his 'partners'" (VD 22). The covenants in the Bible, therefore, are concrete expressions of God's desire for an intimate and enduring relationship with his beloved children, whose response "is love, and loving God means worshipping him."[70]

The Old Testament authors used different images to explain the distinctive nature of God's Covenant with his people. These images—a father and child, a husband and wife, a shepherd and his flock—give us a richer understanding of this covenant relationship. First, the Covenant between God and his people is a relationship of filial love, devotion, and obedience, like the relationship of a *father and child.* "For I have become a father to Israel" (Jer 31:9), declares the Lord, to which Israel replies, "You, O LORD, are our father" (Is 63:16). Second, the Covenant was also compared to the committed love and fidelity of a *husband and wife.* Through the prophet Hosea God promised Israel, "I will take you for my wife forever; I will take you for my wife in righteousness and in justice, in steadfast love, and in mercy. I will take you for my wife in faithfulness; and you shall know the LORD" (2:19–20). Third, the Covenant includes the protective care of the *shepherd for his flock.* During Israel's exile in Babylon, God promised, "I myself will be the shepherd of my sheep . . . I will seek the lost, and I will bring back the strayed, and I will bind up the injured, and I will strengthen the weak, but the fat and the strong I will destroy" (Ez 34:15–16). And in the well-known Twenty-Third Psalm David professes, "The LORD is my shepherd, I shall not want" (Ps 23:1). God was Israel's loving father, faithful spouse, and caring shepherd.

Each of these images is fulfilled in Christ. First, in Christ we are *children* of God the Father. God sent his Son, writes

Saint Paul, "so that we might receive adoption as children. And because you are children, God has sent the Spirit of his Son into our hearts, crying, 'Abba! Father!'" (Gal 4:5–6). Second, the Letter to the Ephesians explains how Christ's relationship with the Church is reflected in the committed love and fidelity of *marriage*. "This is a great mystery," wrote Saint Paul, referring to marriage, "and I am applying it to Christ and the church" (Eph 5:32).

> Christ loved the church and gave himself up for her, in order to make her holy by cleansing her with the washing of water by the word, so as to present the church to himself in splendor, without a spot or wrinkle or anything of the kind—yes, so that she may be holy and without blemish. (Eph 5:25–27)

Third, the New Covenant is characterized by the vigilant and sacrificial care of the *shepherd*. Jesus taught his disciples, "I am the good shepherd. The good shepherd lays down his life for the sheep" (Jn 10:11). He is "the great shepherd of the sheep" (Heb 13:20). The New Covenant unites us to Christ, who is our brother, our spouse, and our eternal shepherd. This brings us to our second question.

How Did the Old Testament Covenants Prefigure the New Covenant?

The Old Testament recounts God's progressive revelation of himself to his people. The revelation of the divine name to Moses in the burning bush (see Ex 3:14) was "the fundamental one for both the Old and the New Covenants" (CCC 204). This revelation initiated a relationship that led to Israel's deliverance from Egypt—the Exodus.

When God led Israel out of Egypt into the desert, he bound himself to his people with a Covenant on Mount Sinai called the Mosaic Covenant. "From the covenant of Sinai onwards, this people is 'his own' and it is to be a 'holy nation,' because the name of God dwells in it" (CCC 2810). The Sinai Covenant is recounted in Exodus chapters 19–24: God manifested his glory on Mount Sinai (see Ex 19), gave the Ten Commandments (see Ex 20), stipulated the requirements of the Covenant (see Ex 21–23), promised his blessings and protection (see Ex 23), and ratified the Covenant (see Ex 24).

The ratification of the Mosaic Covenant, described in Exodus 24, consisted of three actions: the reading of the Covenant, a sacrifice that sealed the Covenant, and a sacrificial banquet that completed the sacrifice. First, Moses recorded the words of the Lord (v. 4) and read the book of the Covenant aloud to the people (v. 7). Then he built an altar, sacrificed young bulls "as offerings of well-being to the LORD" (v. 5), and then splashed the altar (a symbol of God) and the people with the blood, symbolically uniting God and his people by the blood of the same victim, thus ratifying the Covenant, and told them, "See the blood of the covenant that the LORD has made with you in accordance with all these words" (v. 8). Blood was an essential element because "the life of the flesh is in the blood . . . it is the blood that makes atonement" (Lev 17:11). Finally, Moses ascended Mount Sinai with Aaron, Nadab, Abihu, and seventy elders, where "they ate and drank" (Ex 24:11).

The three elements of the Mosaic Covenant prefigured the definitive Covenant in Christ's Blood. "By analogy with the Covenant of Mount Sinai, sealed by sacrifice and the sprinkling of blood," explained Saint John Paul II, "the actions and words of Jesus at the Last Supper laid the foundations of the new messianic community, the People of the New Covenant" (EE 21). On the night of his betrayal and passion, Jesus gathers his apostles in the Upper Room. He washes their feet and gives them the new "Law" of the New Covenant—to love each other as he loved them. And he celebrates the Last Supper with them, instituting the Eucharist—the *sacrifice* and *banquet* of the New Covenant. He first gives the apostles his Body under the appearance of bread. He then gives them the chalice of his Blood with these words: "Drink from it, all of you [*banquet*]; for this is my *blood* of the *covenant*, which is poured out [*sacrifice*] for many for the forgiveness of sins" (Mt 26:27–28; emphasis added). The essential elements from Exodus 24 are now definitively fulfilled by Christ: the terms of the Covenant are proclaimed, it is sealed with the Blood of the pure sacrificial Victim, and it is consummated by a sacred banquet.

Why did Jesus speak of this as a "new" Covenant? To answer this question, we must turn again to the Old Testament. Israel was repeatedly unfaithful to the Mosaic Covenant, and as a result the prophets rebuked Israel. God, however, never abandoned his people. "Through the prophets, God forms his people in the hope of salvation, in the expectation of a new and everlasting Covenant intended for all, to be written on their hearts" (CCC 64). God spoke of this New Covenant through the prophet Jeremiah. "I will make a new covenant with the house of Israel and the house of Judah.... I will put my law within them, and I will write it on their hearts; and I will be their God, and they shall be my people" (Jer 31:31, 33). The New Testament itself explains that this prophecy was fulfilled by the once-for-all sacrifice of Christ (see Heb 10:12–18). We are now ready to look in detail at our third question.

How Is the Covenant Renewed in the Mass?

At the Last Supper, Christ, "the *true* paschal lamb who freely gave himself in sacrifice for us, and thus brought about the new and eternal Covenant" (SacCar 9), instituted the sacramental commemoration of his sacrifice and commanded his disciples to celebrate it until his return. The three essential elements identified above in the Mosaic Covenant and fulfilled at the Last Supper form the basic structure of the Mass. There is the *announcement* of the New Covenant in the Liturgy of the Word, the *renewal of the Covenant sacrifice* in the Eucharistic Prayer, and the *consummation of the Covenant* in the Eucharistic banquet. Although the Mass consists of these distinct parts, it is, nevertheless, one unified act of worship. "The celebration of Mass in which the word is *heard* and the Eucharist is *offered* and *received* forms but one single act of divine worship,"[71] the renewal of God's Covenant with his people and the generous bestowal of his blessings. We will now walk through the renewal of the New Covenant in the Mass, beginning with the announcement of the Covenant in the Liturgy of the Word.

The Covenant Is Announced:
The Liturgy of the Word

The renewal of the Covenant in the Mass begins with the announcement of the Covenant in the Liturgy of the Word. This prepares for and leads to "the *sacrifice* of the New Covenant and the *banquet* of grace, that is, the Eucharist."[72] The Liturgy of the Word for Sunday begins with an Old Testament reading and a responsorial psalm that in some way relates to the Gospel of the day, followed by a reading from one of the New Testament epistles. It culminates in the proclamation of the Gospel. This arrangement of readings has two purposes. First, it "brings out the unity of the Old and New Testaments and of the history of salvation, in which Christ is the central figure, commemorated in his paschal mystery."[73] Second, it makes clear "that the history of salvation is continued here and now in the representation of Christ's paschal mystery celebrated through the Eucharist"[74]—the Mass is the sacramental continuation of God's saving work.

The proclamation of the word "in the Liturgy is always . . . a living and effective word through the power of the Holy Spirit. It expresses the Father's love that never fails in its effectiveness toward us."[75] The power of God's word is known as the *performative* character of the word—it performs or accomplishes what it says—for "there is no separation between what God *says* and what he *does*" (VD 53). There are numerous examples of this in Sacred Scripture. God spoke the world into existence—"God said, 'Let there be light'; and there was light" (Gen 1:3). No other action was necessary.

During his earthly ministry Jesus by a word cast out demons (see Mt 8:32), calmed the storm at sea (see Mt 8:26), caused a fig tree to wither (see Mt 21:19), and changed bread and wine into his Body and Blood at the Last Supper (see Mt 26:26–28).

The Liturgy of the Word is the joint work of the Father, the Son, and the Holy Spirit. In the Scriptures the Father speaks to his children, and Jesus, the Word of the Father, proclaims the Gospel. The Holy Spirit "brings home to each person individually everything that in the proclamation of the word of God is spoken for the good of the whole gathering of the faithful" and is able "to make what we hear outwardly have its effect inwardly."[76] The proclamation of the word of God's New Covenant requires a response, and so the assembly "must respond to that word in faith, so that they may become more and more truly the people of the New Covenant."[77]

Nurturing Eucharistic Amazement

Our encounter with God in the Mass is a dialogue in which he speaks and we respond. In the Liturgy of the Word he speaks through the Scriptures, and it is significant that the Church recommends periods of silence after he has spoken to us in the readings and the homily. This silence is not just time to think about what has been heard. It is a time for God to act, for the Holy Spirit to speak and to apply the word proclaimed in a personal and individual way to each person. And it is a time to respond to the Spirit. It is a time for silent but authentic conversation with God, to invite and accept, to question and answer, to share love. It is a time when God may teach, heal, challenge, console, free, or forgive because, by the working of the Holy Spirit, his word is always capable of accomplishing what it says. You can prepare for this encounter by looking over the readings before Mass, which can be found in a daily missal or online.

The Sacrifice of the Covenant: The Liturgy of the Eucharist

The proclamation of the Covenant in the Liturgy of the Word leads to the Liturgy of the Eucharist, "the very offering through which Christ has confirmed the New Covenant in his Blood."[78] At the Last Supper Jesus spoke of his impending death as a sacrifice. He offered his disciples his Body "which is given for you" and his Blood "that is poured out for you" (Lk 22:19–20)—he is not offering them just his Body and Blood, but the *sacrifice* of his Body "given" and his Blood "poured out." At the Last Supper he "anticipated his death and resurrection by giving his disciples, in the bread and wine, his very self, his Body and Blood as the new manna (see Jn 6:31–33)."[79] Let's look more closely at the biblical understanding of sacrifice.

Sacrifice: Gift, Healing, Communion

Sacrifice was about relationship—the establishment of a relationship, the healing of a wounded relationship, and the strengthening of the individual's and the community's relationship with God. It was "the central act of Israelite worship"[80] and consisted of three essential aspects: gift, expiation, and communion.[81] The sacrifice was a *gift*, but a gift that itself came from God and was being returned to God. "For everything is from you," David prayed, "and what we give is what we have from you" (1 Chr 29:14 NABRE). The gifts were necessities of life and so were an expression of one's life and oneself. The second aspect of sacrifice was *expiation*, the healing and restoration of a damaged relationship: "all sacrifice tended to establish good relations between God and man."[82] The third aspect of sacrifice was *communion*. In many of the sacrifices, a portion was reserved for God while the remainder was consumed by those who presented the offering, signifying that the sacrifice "brought the two parties together in a spiritual communion, establishing and consolidating the covenant bond between the two."[83] It was "regarded as the most complete kind of sacrifice."[84]

Christ's sacrificial death on the cross definitively fulfilled the three aspects of sacrifice. First, Christ did not offer his Father a gift of an animal or vegetable sacrifice, he offered himself to the Father. Christ himself was the *gift*: Christ "through the eternal Spirit offered himself without blemish to God" (Heb 9:14). Second, Christ's sacrifice offered in expiation *healed our broken relationship*. Christ "gave himself for our sins" (Gal 1:4) as "the *sacrifice of the New Covenant*," restoring us "to communion with God by reconciling [us] . . . through the 'blood of the covenant, which was poured out for many for the forgiveness of sins'" (CCC 613). Third, Christ's sacrifice fulfilled the Old Testament sacrifice of *communion*. In the Eucharistic banquet we receive Christ's Body and Blood that "brings about in a sublime way the mutual 'abiding' of Christ and each of his followers: 'Abide in me as I in you' (Jn 15:4)" (EE 22).

How is the sacrifice of the Mass related to the sacrifice on Calvary? Christ's sacrifice on Calvary and his sacrifice in the Mass "are *one single sacrifice*: 'The victim is one and the same . . . the same Christ who offered himself once in a bloody manner on the altar of the cross is contained and offered in an unbloody manner'" in the Mass.[85] Christ is both the one who *offers* and the one who *is offered*, both on Calvary and in the Mass. At the same time, Christ is the one who is offered, and the Body of Christ offered on the cross and the Body offered in the Eucharist are one and the same Body. The only difference is the manner of offering—on Calvary in his incarnate Body, in the Mass sacramentally under the signs of bread and wine.

The Eucharistic Prayer

The Eucharistic Prayer, which effects the Eucharistic sacrifice, is the Trinity's great action in the world. At this point, human action "steps back and makes way for . . . the action of God. . . . God himself acts and does what is essential."[86] What precisely does God do? What is happening in this great prayer? The Eucharistic Prayer is addressed to God the Father, but it is the joint work of the three Persons of the Trinity. The priest, holding his hands over the bread and wine, prays that the Holy Spirit would come upon them and change them into the Body and Blood of Christ. Then Christ, through the priest, speaks the words of Consecration: "This is my Body," "This is my Blood."[87] Saint John Chrysostom explained the mystery of this moment: "The priest, in the role of Christ, pronounces these words, but their power and grace are God's. This is my body, he says. This word transforms the things offered."[88] By Christ's words and actions, and the working of the Holy Spirit, the bread and wine are transubstantiated into the Body and Blood of Christ. Christ is now fully present on the altar, doing under sacramental signs all that he did during his earthly ministry. Together with Christ and his Church, the priest and the assembly offer to the Father "in thanksgiving this holy and living sacrifice."[89] We include ourselves in this offering, for the Church desires that we, participating in offering "the unblemished sacrificial Victim," will also learn to offer ourselves "and so day by day to be brought, through the mediation of Christ, into unity with God and with each other, so that God may at last be all in all."[90] Following this, the Holy Spirit again is invoked, this time upon the assembly, that we "may become one body, one spirit in Christ."[91]

Intercessions are then offered for those present, the universal Church, and the world. We ask God to "listen graciously to the prayers" of the assembly and to make the congregation "an eternal offering" to him. We pray that the sacrifice just accomplished will "advance the peace and salvation of all the world," and we ask the Lord to "confirm in faith and charity your pilgrim Church on earth."[92] We always pray that God would welcome our deceased brethren into his presence. In the words of Saint Cyril of Jerusalem, we do this because "we have a deep conviction that great help will be afforded those souls for whom prayers are offered while this holy and awesome Victim is present."[93] The Eucharistic Prayer concludes with the doxology in which we offer all honor and glory through, with, and in Christ, in the unity of the Holy Spirit, to the Father. The people's response—"Amen"—is their assent to all that has been proclaimed and accomplished in the Eucharistic Prayer.

The Eucharistic Prayer is the Trinity's supreme action in the world that makes sacramentally present the sacrifice of the new eternal Covenant. The entire prayer is addressed to God the Father. The Holy Spirit is invoked over the bread and wine, Christ speaks the words of institution—"This is my Body," "This is my Blood"—through the mouth of the priest, and we unite ourselves with Christ and the Church in his self-offering in the Spirit to the Father. The Holy Spirit comes down "to make the saving work of Christ present and active by his transforming power; and to make the gift of communion bear fruit in the Church" (CCC 1112). The graces announced in the Liturgy of the Word are made present in the Eucharistic sacrifice. This brings us to the consummation of the Covenant, the banquet.

Nurturing Eucharistic Amazement

The laity—you—can interiorly participate in the Eucharistic Prayer. Although said by the priest, you are invited to join with Christ in proclaiming God's wondrous works by giving interior assent to what is proclaimed.

- ✦ When the priest says the words of the offering, "we offer you," the "we" includes you. When you hear these words, intentionally include yourself, for this is an important moment for you to deepen your relationship with both God and the People of God.

- ✦ Studying and meditating on one or more Eucharistic Prayers can also deepen your participation at Mass and enrich your personal prayer.

The Covenant Banquet— The Communion Rite

Christ's new and eternal Covenant, announced in the Liturgy of the Word and effected by the Eucharistic sacrifice, is now completed in the sacrificial banquet. In the words of the *Catechism*, "the celebration of the Eucharistic sacrifice is wholly directed toward the intimate union of the faithful with Christ through communion. To receive communion is to receive Christ himself who has offered himself for us" (CCC 1382). The transforming power of the sacrifice comes to us in Communion, as Pope Francis explained: "When we receive him in Holy Communion, we renew our Covenant with him and allow him to carry out ever more fully his work of transforming our lives."[94]

We prepare for Communion with a prayer that acknowledges our unworthiness but also our faith in Christ's mercy and power—"Lord, I am not worthy that you should enter under my roof, but only say the word and my soul shall be healed."[95] This prayer is from the Gospels—the reply of the Roman centurion to Jesus' offer to come to his home to heal his servant (see Mt 8:8). Jesus praised his faith and said, "Go; let it be done for you according to your faith" (Mt 8:13). And with that word the centurion's servant was healed. We now receive our Eucharistic Lord, completing our renewal of the New Covenant.

Nurturing Eucharistic Amazement

After the Lamb of God, the priest quietly says one of two prayers in preparation for his own Communion. The second option includes a petition for his own healing. Then all say the prayer of the Roman centurion, which is a prayer for the healing of our soul. After Communion is completed, during the purification of the vessels, the priest quietly says a prayer that asks that the Eucharist just received may bring eternal healing. Three prayers, before and after Communion, all asking for healing!

These prayers for healing in the Communion Rite reveal what God is doing at this moment. Healing takes many forms, and you may not even know what kind of healing you need. The Lord whom you have just received, however, does know. This can be a time for the simplest of prayers: Jesus, heal me. Jesus, have mercy. Jesus, I love you.

———————————•———————————

Conclusion

God, whose character is always to bless, has united us to himself by an eternal Covenant through the Blood of Christ that fulfills and surpasses all of the covenants of the Old Testament. It was accomplished by the joint working of the Trinity: Christ through the eternal Spirit offered himself without blemish to the Father (see Heb 9:14). The renewal of the Covenant in the Eucharist is a single act of worship that begins with the proclamation of the Covenant in which God speaks to his people, Christ proclaims his Gospel, and the Holy Spirit communicates the word personally to each individual. The proclamation of the Covenant leads to the sacrifice of the Covenant in which Christ becomes present through his word and the power of the Spirit. The Covenant renewal is completed by the sacrificial banquet in which we are nourished by Christ's Body and Blood and filled with the Holy Spirit so that we become one in Christ. Through our union with Christ, we receive an increase in divine light and life for our own good and the good of the Church and the world.

NOTES

69. Joseph Ratzinger, *Spirit of the Liturgy*, 26.

70. Joseph Ratzinger, *Spirit of the Liturgy*, 26.

71. *Lectionary for Mass for Use in the Dioceses of the United States of America*, Second Typical Edition, "Introduction to the Lectionary" (Washington, DC: Confraternity of Christian Doctrine, 2001, 1998, 1997, 1970), 10. Italics added.

72. *Lectionary for Mass*, 10. Italics added.

73. *Lectionary for Mass*, 66.1.

74. *Lectionary for Mass*, 61.

75. *Lectionary for Mass*, 4.

76. *Lectionary for Mass*, 9.

77. *Lectionary for Mass*, 45.

78. *Lectionary for Mass*, 44.

79. Benedict XVI, *Deus Caritas Est* (Boston: Pauline Books & Media, 2005), 13.

80. Raymond E. Brown, Joseph Fitzmyer, and Roland Murphy, eds., *New Jerome Biblical Commentary* (Upper Saddle River: Prentice Hall, 1990), 1268.

81. See Brown, Fitzmyer, and Murphy, eds., *New Jerome Biblical Commentary*, 1272.

82. Roland de Vaux, O.P., *Ancient Israel: Its Life and Institutions*, trans. John McHugh (Grand Rapids: William B. Eerdmans and Livonia: Dove Booksellers, 1997), 453.

83. Brown, Fitzmyer, and Murphy, eds., *New Jerome Biblical Commentary*, 1273.

84. De Vaux, *Ancient Israel: Its Life and Institutions*, 453.

85. *Catechism of the Catholic Church*, 1367 [Council of Trent (1562) *Doctrina de ss. Missae sacrificio*, c. 2: DS 1743; cf. Heb 9:14, 27].

86. Ratzinger, *Spirit of the Liturgy*, 172–73.

87. See *Roman Missal*, Order of Mass (EP III) 110, 111.

88. *Catechism of the Catholic Church*, 1375 [St. John Chrysostom, *prod. Jud.* 1:6: PG 49, 380].

89. *Roman Missal*, Order of Mass (EP III) 113.

90. USCCB, *General Instruction of the Roman Missal* (GIRM), USCCB Liturgy Documentary Series 14 (Washington, DC: United States Conference of Catholic Bishops, 2010), para 79.

91. *Roman Missal*, Order of Mass (EP III) 113.

92. *Roman Missal*, Order of Mass (EP III) 113.

93. Paul VI, *Mysterium Fidei*, 30 [*Catecheses*, 23 [*myst.* 5]. 8–18; PG 33.1115–1118].

94. Francis, *Gaudete et Exsultate* (Boston: Pauline Books & Media, 2018), 157.

95. *Roman Missal*, Order of Mass 132.

CHAPTER 5

Christ's Mysteries
Made Present

The chief function of the liturgy is to bring us divine life
now.

PIUS PARSCH, *THE CHURCH'S YEAR OF GRACE*

OUR COVENANT WITH GOD is renewed in the Mass,
drawing us into the love of the Trinity and bestowing
on us God's blessings. Healing, peace, guidance, and theological insight were some of the blessings Saint Teresa of Avila
received at Mass. Her experiences illustrate an important
aspect of the Mass, that each celebration of the Eucharist
makes present specific graces.

When God's saving events are celebrated in the liturgy,
"they become in a certain way present and real. This is how
Israel understands its liberation from Egypt: every time

Passover is celebrated, the Exodus events are made present to the memory of believers so that they may conform their lives to them" (CCC 1363). For the Israelites, the Passover and other major festivals like Weeks and Tents were "reenactments of Yahweh's saving deeds, and by their celebration the saving power and will of Yahweh are experienced anew."[96] The Church uses the term *memorial* to describe this power of the liturgy to make *present* and *real* God's saving acts.

The Old Testament understanding of *memorial* received its new and definitive meaning in the New Testament. At the Last Supper Christ "instituted the Eucharist as the memorial of his death and Resurrection, and commanded his apostles to celebrate it until his return" (CCC 1337). Christ "wanted us to have the memorial of the love with which he loved us 'to the end,' even to the giving of his life" (CCC 1380). Christ's entire earthly ministry, culminating in his suffering, death, and resurrection, abides for all eternity and is made present until his return: "All that Christ is—all that he did and suffered for all men—participates in the divine eternity, and so transcends all times while being made present in them all" (CCC 1085). When each of Christ's saving mysteries, from the annunciation to Mary to his ascension, is celebrated in the liturgy, it is made sacramentally present.

While the Church has always believed that the Eucharist makes sacramentally present the mysteries of Christ's life, it was neglected in her teaching, although not in the experience of the faithful, as we have seen with Saint Teresa of Avila. The nineteenth and twentieth centuries brought a rediscovery of this truth. In this chapter we will look at some of the key figures and events in this rediscovery—two monks, a pope, an ecumenical council, and a catechism. We will begin with Prosper Guéranger, "one of the first modern writers to restate the traditional teaching of the Church on the liturgy. . . . His work was truly prophetic."[97]

The Power of the Special Grace— Prosper Guéranger

Prosper Louis Pascal Guéranger (1805–1875) was a French priest who reestablished the Benedictine Abbey of Solesmes in 1833. In 1841 he began writing *The Liturgical Year*, a commentary on the texts of the Mass and the Divine Office (the Church's official prayer) that drew on history, the Church Fathers, Eastern and Western liturgical traditions, and the liturgical rites themselves. Guéranger taught that "the liturgical year is presented by the Church in such a way that each mystery or feast celebrated during the course of the year brings its own *particular grace* and insight, a grace which is actualized in the given celebration."[98] He intended this work to "be unlike any hitherto published work on the liturgical year."[99]

In his preface to *The Liturgical Year*, Guéranger stated his fundamental conviction:

> The ecclesiastical year, which we have undertaken to explain in this work, is neither more nor less than the manifestation of Jesus Christ and his mysteries, in the Church and in the faithful soul. It is the divine cycle, in which appear all the works of God, each in its turn.[100]

In the course of the liturgical year, "the Church renews her youth as that of the eagle (see Ps 102, 5) . . . because . . . she is visited by her divine Spouse, who supplies all her wants."[101] This is true not only "for the Church at large . . . [but] also for the soul of each one of the faithful that is careful to receive the gift of God," for the succession of seasons and feasts "imparts to the Christian the elements of that supernatural life, without which every other life is but a sort of death, more or less disguised."[102] The mysteries of Christ's life—his conception, birth, public ministry, and paschal mystery—are granted to us "by the power of the special grace which the liturgy produces,"[103] making us more and more like Jesus.

A significant aspect of Guéranger's work was his understanding of the work of the Holy Spirit in the liturgy. The manifestation of Jesus Christ and his mysteries in the Mass, he wrote, "is a mystery of the Holy Ghost," who effects "a twofold growth . . . the increase of knowledge of the truths of faith, and the development of the supernatural life."[104] Guéranger's goal was to enable the faithful to discern the work of the Holy Spirit throughout the liturgical year and so experience the power of the liturgy's special grace in every feast and season.

To introduce the faithful to the power of the liturgy, Guéranger carefully explained the antiphons, prayers, and readings of the Mass, showing how they reveal different aspects of each celebration and suggesting the specific graces offered in each celebration. As an example of his approach, we will look at his catechesis on the Christmas Mass During the Night. He begins by explaining two different aspects of the birth of Jesus. First, he describes the relationship between Christ's coming at Christmas and his coming in the Eucharist. "It is now time to offer the Great Sacrifice [the Eucharist], and to call down our Emmanuel from heaven. . . . He will intercede for us on the altar, as he did in his crib. We will approach him with love, and he will give himself to us." Second, Guéranger explains that Christ's first coming is the work of the Trinity: "God the *Father* has given his *Son* to us; and it is by the operation of the *Holy Ghost* that the grand portent is produced."

Guéranger then sets the scene, describing the events that occurred two thousand years ago and which now, in their liturgical celebration, are happening "today." He begins, "At Bethlehem, round the stable, and in the city, all is deep darkness; and the inhabitants, who would not find room for the divine Babe, are sleeping heavily: will they awaken when the angels begin to sing?" Christ is born, and Mary experiences "her first sight of her Son, who is Son also of the Eternal Father! She adores . . . and lays him down in the manger. Her faithful Joseph unites his adoration with hers; and so, too, do the angels of heaven." What is the assembly's response? "The eyes of the faithful are now riveted on the sanctuary, where the same Jesus is to be their Holy Sacrifice."

The entrance antiphon, which introduces the Mass, is a prophecy from Psalm 2:7: "The Lord said to me: You are my Son. It is I who have begotten you this day." This Mass commemorates the fulfillment of this prophecy. In the Gloria the assembly joins in the praise of the heavenly host, present now as then:

> These our heavenly brethren first intoned it, and they are, at this moment, round our altar, as they were round the crib; they are singing our happiness. . . . Oh! yes; let us all,

men and angels, Church of earth and Church of heaven, let us sing: *Glory be to God! and Peace to men!*[105]

The opening prayer praises God for making "this most sacred night radiant with the splendor of the true light" and asks that all "who have known the mysteries of his light on the earth may also delight in his gladness in heaven."[106]

The first reading is Titus 2:11–14, which tells us that Christ appeared in the flesh to save us and teach us to live holy lives as we await his second coming. This, too, is happening now, says Guéranger. The Gospel is Luke's account of the birth, Luke 2:1–14, and its proclamation moved Guéranger from catechesis to prayer: "Praise be to thee, sweetest Jesus, for thy mercy! and love from all hearts for thy tender love of us! Our eyes are riveted on that dear crib, for our salvation is there." On this night the Creed is recited with an added gesture—at the words of his incarnation of the Virgin Mary by the Holy Spirit, all kneel to "profoundly adore the great God who assumed our human nature, and became like unto us, his poor creatures; let your adoration and love repay him, if it were possible, for this his incomprehensible abasement."

In his commentary on the Eucharistic Prayer, Guéranger gives special attention to the priest's elevation of the Host and chalice following the Consecration.

At the Elevation, when, in the midst of the mysterious silence, your Savior, the Incarnate Word, descends upon the altar, you must see, with the eye of your faith, the crib, and Jesus stretching out his hands to his Eternal Father, and looking upon you with extreme tenderness, and Mary adoring him with a Mother's love, and Joseph looking on and weeping with joy, and the holy angels lost in amazement at the mystery.

He encouraged the assembly to respond generously to this great mystery. "You must give your heart to the newborn Babe, that he may fill it with what he wishes to see there; nay, beg of him to fill it with himself, and make himself its Master and its all." The celebration culminates in sacramental Communion, in which we are "united to the Infant God."[107] The Mass concludes with a prayer that God's people would be drawn into closer union with Christ.

Guéranger's commentary on the Christmas Mass During the Night illustrates his approach to liturgical catechesis in *The Liturgical Year*: the event being celebrated is happening now, "today"; all that is done is the joint work of the Trinity; the liturgical celebration communicates the special graces of the event being commemorated; and attention to the prayers and readings proper to the celebration will reveal its special graces. These are aspects of the liturgy that Guéranger's successors will continue to explore.

The Liturgy Brings Us Divine Life Now— Pius Parsch

The next liturgical pioneer we will explore is Dr. Pius Parsch (1884–1954), a canon of the Augustinian monastery at Klosterneuburg near Vienna. Parsch wrote a multivolume commentary on the liturgical year, *The Church's Year of Grace*, which he completed in 1929. It was translated into English and published in the United States between the years 1953 and 1959. "We must grasp one thing: the liturgy is primarily concerned with the present," he wrote in the introduction. "The past and the future are only symbols or signposts of today's outpouring of grace. The chief function of the liturgy is to bring *us* divine life *now*."[108]

Each celebration of the Eucharist, taught Parsch, makes present unique—"peculiar"—graces. "The sacrifice of Mass offered on various feasts and weekdays actualized the sacred event commemorated," he wrote, "making present its *peculiar* graces."[109] He affirmed the fullness of Christ's presence in the liturgy. "For in the Mass not only are the Body and Blood of Christ present, but the divine High Priest and Lamb of God appears on the altar, fulfilling there the symbols of his earthly life." Furthermore, the liturgy transcends time so that past and future converge on today. Parsch wrote,

> Through the Eucharist history becomes present and hope becomes reality. The past and future become actual here before our eyes. What we read as past history and what we await as future hope merge into a holy *now* and a holy *today* in the Mass.[110]

As an example of Parsch's method of liturgical catechesis, we will look at his commentary on the Feast of the Transfiguration. He begins with the Liturgy of the Word, in which the event of the transfiguration is proclaimed, beginning with Saint Peter's account (see 2 Pet 1) and culminating in the proclamation of the Gospel in which we see the transfigured Christ. In the Liturgy of the Eucharist, the Prayer over the Offerings "voices our plea that the 'splendor of his transfiguration cleanse away the stains of our sins' (as the sun dissipates diseases)." Then, "by means of the sacrifice proper and especially the sacred banquet, the transfiguration becomes an actuality through the sacrament; the glorified Christ appears and we are sharers of his glory. . . . Holy Mass is our hour on Tabor." Like Peter, James, and John, we leave Mass changed. As we return "to our places of work in the world, we carry along the graces received in the inmost sanctuary of our hearts."[111]

The transfiguration is one of the great mysteries of Jesus' earthly ministry, but Parsch also possessed a deep insight into "the import of the transfiguration to the liturgy itself." He said that every celebration of the Mass is the event of the transfiguration under sacramental signs.

> What once happened during the night on Mount Tabor happens again every time the holy sacrifice is offered. We may see only the simple appearances upon the altar, but with the eyes of faith we behold the glorified Christ; we see, in fact, the King of glory with his court, the saints of the Old and New Covenant. Liturgy actualizes in our very presence the sanctifying act of Christ at his transfiguration.

The transfiguration reveals the ultimate goal of the Christian life that occurs in the Eucharist. "It is, therefore, not only Christ who becomes transfigured—he allows me to share his glory. . . . The purpose of the liturgy is the divine transfiguration of the participants." Parsch quoted a passage from Philippians to explain the event that is anticipated by the transfiguration: when Christ returns, "he will transform the body of our humiliation that it may be conformed to the body of his glory" (Phil 3:21). The Mass is nothing less than "the sacrament of transfiguration, for it is 'the seed of glory.'"[112]

Parsch's work echoed the work of Guéranger in many ways. Both wrote detailed commentaries on the liturgical year. Both emphasized that in the liturgical celebration the event being commemorated becomes present and real through the sacrament, that every saving event becomes "a holy *now* and a holy *today* in the Mass."[113] And both taught that each celebration of the Mass made present special graces. We turn now to a major papal contribution to the liturgical renewal.

Journey of Immense Mercy—Pius XII

In 1947 Pope Pius XII wrote the first encyclical devoted entirely to the liturgy, *Mediator Dei*. It was a pivotal moment for the Church. The teaching is familiar, echoing that of Guéranger and Parsch, but the voice is different—now it is the official voice of holy Mother Church addressing her children. The liturgical year is nothing less than "Christ himself who is ever living in his Church."[114] Christ's saving words and works "are ever present and active," and "each mystery brings its own special grace for our salvation" (MD 165). In the course of the liturgical year, Christ is sacramentally present

> as the Word of the eternal Father, as born of the Virgin Mother of God, as he who teaches us truth, heals the sick, consoles the afflicted, who endures suffering and who dies; finally, as he who rose triumphantly from the dead and who, reigning in the glory of heaven, sends us the Holy

Paraclete and who abides in his Church forever. (MD 163)

The Mass, taught Pius XII, is a personal encounter with Christ, whom we meet

> not only as a model to be imitated but as a Master to whom we should listen readily, a Shepherd whom we should follow, Author of our salvation, the Source of our holiness and the Head of the Mystical Body whose members we are, living by his very life. (MD 163)

In the liturgical year, Christ

> continues that journey of immense mercy which he lovingly began in his mortal life, going about doing good, with the design of bringing men to know his mysteries and in a way live by them. These mysteries are ever present and active . . . they still influence us.

When we approach the Eucharistic Christ, "we can receive from him living vitality as branches do from the tree and members from the Head" (MD 165) so that we may grow "'to the measure of the full stature of Christ' (Eph 4:13)" (MD 165).

Riches Made Present—Vatican Council II

In 1963 the Second Vatican Council (1962–1965) produced the first of its sixteen major documents, the *Constitution on the Sacred Liturgy* (*Sacrosanctum Concilium*), signaling by its priority as well as its teaching the preeminence of the liturgy in the life of the Church. In the liturgy we have "access to the stream of divine grace which flows from the paschal mystery of the passion, death, the resurrection of Christ, the font from which all sacraments and sacramentals draw their power" (SC 61). Over the course of the liturgical year the Church "unfolds the whole mystery of Christ, from the incarnation and birth until the ascension, the day of Pentecost, and the expectation of blessed hope and of the coming of the Lord" (SC 102). Moreover, the Council affirmed that the celebrations of the mysteries of Christ make present their special graces. In the liturgical celebration of the events of our salvation "the Church opens to the faithful the riches of her Lord's powers and merits, so that these are in some way *made present in every age;* the faithful *lay hold of them* and *are filled with saving grace*" (SC 102; CCC 1163; italics added). The fullness of the Father's revelation in Christ through the Holy Spirit is made present and its power communicated to us.

The "Today" of Her Liturgy— *Catechism of the Catholic Church*

In the years following the Second Vatican Council the Church has continued to reflect on and deepen her understanding of the Council's teaching, presenting it in the *Catechism of the Catholic Church*. The liturgy does more than recall God's saving works, it "actualizes them, makes them present" (CCC 1104). A key word for the liturgy is "today." "When the Church celebrates the mystery of Christ," says the *Catechism*, "there is a word that marks her prayer: 'Today!'—a word echoing the prayer her Lord taught her and the call of the Holy Spirit" (CCC 1165). In the course of the liturgical year "the Church, especially during Advent and Lent and above all at the Easter Vigil, re-reads and re-lives the great events of salvation history in the 'today' of her liturgy" (CCC 1095).

The Church has continued to deepen her understanding of the role of the Holy Spirit in the liturgy. According to the *Catechism*, "in each celebration there is an outpouring of the Holy Spirit that makes the unique mystery present" (CCC 1104). In addition, the *Catechism* emphasizes the need for the kind of catechesis we encounter in Guéranger and Parsch. Reliving the events of our salvation in the "today" of the liturgy "demands that catechesis help the faithful to open themselves to this spiritual understanding of the economy of salvation as the Church's liturgy reveals it and enables us to live it" (CCC 1095).

Nurturing Eucharistic Amazement

The liturgical year is an important factor in Eucharistic amazement. It begins with Advent and continues through Christmas, the beginning of Ordinary Time, Lent, and Easter, and concludes with Ordinary Time. It is expressed in the Mass in a number of ways, including different colors, changes in the music, variations in the decoration of the church, and the choice of readings, all of which influence our experience of and participation in the Mass.

✦ Before walking through the liturgical year with Saint Faustina in the next chapter, it may be helpful to reflect on a few questions. How does your parish celebrate the different seasons? What are your favorite seasons of the liturgical year? What are the most important feast days for you? Do you prepare for the different seasons of the Church's year? Have you experienced particular graces during certain seasons or on specific feast days? Do you do anything as a family for the different seasons and feasts? Do you remember observing them when you were growing up?

✦ A great way to bring the liturgical year into the home is by setting up a home or family altar or a prayer corner. A "home altar starter kit" could include a Bible, crucifix, rosary, and candle. During the liturgical year various items could be added, such as icons, prayer cards, a cloth or runner that is the color of the liturgical season, and devotions specific to the season being celebrated. Home altars can contribute greatly to the family's faith and prayer.

Conclusion

Through the work of monks, a pope, a council, and a catechism over the past two centuries, the Church has affirmed her perennial teaching on the power and distinctive graces of the Eucharist. In the Eucharist every mystery of our Lord is relived and its power made present. We will now turn to a contemporary of Parsch—a humble Polish nun who experienced in a particular way the special graces of the Mass throughout the liturgical year.

NOTES

96. Brown, Fitzmyer, and Murphy, eds., *New Jerome Biblical Commentary*, 1300.

97. Cuthbert Johnson, "The Pastoral Power of the Liturgy: Prosper Guéranger's Année Liturgique," *Ephemerides Liturgicae*, Anno CXXII, 2008, 240–49, 245.

98. Johnson, "The Pastoral Power of the Liturgy," 246. Italics added.

99. Johnson, "The Pastoral Power of the Liturgy," 241–42.

100. Prosper Guéranger, *The Liturgical Year*, trans. Laurence Shepherd, OSB (Fitzwilliam: Loreto Publications, 2013), 1:9.

101. Guéranger, *The Liturgical Year*, 1:10.

102. Guéranger, *The Liturgical Year*, 1:11.

103. Guéranger, *The Liturgical Year*, 1:17.

104. Guéranger, *The Liturgical Year*, 1:16.

105. Guéranger, *The Liturgical Year*, 2:166–69.

106. *Roman Missal*, The Nativity of the Lord [Christmas], At the Mass during the Night, Collect. This Collect is essentially the same (a slight variation in the Latin word order) in the 1962 Missal and the 2010 Missal. Due to the essential similarity in the Collects, Prefaces, and other liturgical texts in the 1962 and 2010 versions of the Roman Missal, all of the titles of feast days and liturgical quotations throughout this book are from the Roman Missal which is currently in use, that is, *The Roman Missal*, English translation according to the Third Typical Edition, 2010.

107. Guéranger, *The Liturgical Year*, 2:172–74.

108. Pius Parsch, *The Church's Year of Grace*, trans. William G. Heidt, OSB (Collegeville: Liturgical Press, 1959), 1:5.

109. Parsch, *The Church's Year of Grace*, 4:10. Italics added.

110. Parsch, *The Church's Year of Grace*, 1:5.

111. Parsch, *The Church's Year of Grace*, 4:301.

112. Parsch, *The Church's Year of Grace*, 4:303.

113. Parsch, *The Church's Year of Grace*, 1:5.

114. Pius XII, *Mediator Dei* (November 20, 1947), The Holy See, Vatican.va, 165. https://www.vatican.va/content/pius-xii/en/encyclicals/documents/hf_p-xii_enc_20111947_mediator-dei.html.

CHAPTER 6

His Divine Love Provides: Saint Faustina

Almost every feast of the Church gives me a deeper knowledge of God and a special grace.

DIARY OF SAINT MARIA FAUSTINA KOWALSKA

MANY SAINTS HAVE EXPERIENCED in the Eucharist the special graces of each liturgical season and feast. In his preaching on the different feasts, the Cistercian monk and mystic Saint Bernard of Clairvaux (†1153) "tried to show the particular graces each feast had for the brothers, and how they could make them their own," because he understood that "it is in the Church and through her liturgical feasts and sacraments that we enter into the mysteries of Christ's earthly life, and share in their redemptive power."[115] It was similar with Saint Teresa of Avila's co-worker and confessor Saint John of the Cross (†1591), as one of his penitents described:

> I noticed that his countenance reflected the feast being celebrated. I became convinced that his heart was set on God in harmony with the feasts and seasons. During the season commemorating the Passion of our Lord Jesus Christ, one could see how this affected him; during the Christmas season, his tender love was obvious. And so it was with the other feasts.[116]

Saint Thérèse of Lisieux (†1897) was introduced from childhood to the graces of each feast, as she lovingly recounted to her sister Pauline (Mother Agnes of Jesus): "How I loved the *feasts!* You knew how to explain all the mysteries hidden under each, and you did it so well that they were truly heavenly days for me."[117]

One saint has left us a particularly detailed account of the special graces she received throughout the liturgical year—Saint Faustina Kowalska. In this chapter we will walk with Saint Faustina through the feasts and seasons of the liturgical year and meditate on her descriptions of the unique graces she received in each.

The Catholic Church possesses a rich treasury of popular piety and devotions such as the Rosary, litanies, novenas, chaplets, and prayers to the saints. As we examine the liturgical year through the experiences of Saint Faustina, suggestions will be made for prayers and devotions appropriate to these different seasons and feasts that can prepare us to participate more fully in Mass and experience more deeply its fruits.

Her Life

Saint Faustina was born Helen Kowalska in 1905, the third of ten children in a poor farming family in Poland. She had only three years of elementary school, and at the age of fourteen began work as domestic help. Although she had first sensed a call to religious life at the age of seven, it wasn't until she was twenty that she entered the Congregation of the Sisters of Our Lady of Mercy in 1925, taking the name Sister Maria Faustina of the Most Blessed Sacrament. She served in the community as a cook, gardener, and gatekeeper. She died of tuberculosis on October 5, 1938. Through this hidden and humble saint the Lord gave the Church the image of the Divine Mercy, the Chaplet of Divine Mercy, and Divine Mercy Sunday (celebrated on the Second Sunday of Easter). She was beatified by Saint John Paul II in 1993 and canonized by him in 2000. Saint Faustina was, he said, "a gift of God to our time."[118]

Faustina recorded her Eucharistic encounters in her diary, which she began in 1934 at the direction of her confessor Father Sopocko. On July 28, 1934, she wrote, "I am to write down the encounters of my soul with you, O God, at the moments of your special visitations."[119] Once, when she did not feel like writing, she heard a voice: "**My daughter, you do not live for yourself but for souls; write for their benefit.**"[120]

Saint Faustina, like Saint Teresa of Avila, often received extraordinary graces from the Lord during Mass. The experiences of these and other saints are one of the ways that God increases our faith in his goodness and power and encourages us to confidently approach the throne of grace (see Phil 4:6

and Heb 4:16). It is important, however, to balance these extraordinary experiences with the advice of Saint John of the Cross regarding the immense value of the invisible graces of the Eucharist. Eucharistic amazement is born from invisible graces as well as extraordinary experiences.

Advent and Christmas

Advent begins the liturgical year. It is the season when the Church recalls and relives Christ's first coming "in the 'today' of her liturgy" (CCC 1095). This is how Faustina understood Advent, as she wrote in her diary: "Advent is approaching. I want to prepare my heart for the coming of the Lord Jesus by silence and recollection of spirit."[121] In her preparation she turned to the Blessed Virgin Mary, imitating her humble silence.

Christmas was one of the most important feasts for Saint Faustina—in her diary she recorded accounts of her experiences during Mass from 1934–1937, the last four years of her life. On Christmas Eve 1934 she experienced a deep union with the Trinity that continued throughout the day. Three years later, her last Christmas on earth, she experienced the Virgin Mary's concern for her infant Son. It had, she said, "such fragrance of abandonment to the will of God that I should call it rather a delight than an anxiety." She concluded that this was a lesson for her: "I understood how my soul ought to accept the will of God in all things."[122]

The Lord granted Faustina many graces during the Christmas Mass During the Night. In 1934 she wrote that at the beginning of Mass she felt great recollection and joy. Then, during the Preparation of the Gifts she described a vision of Jesus "looking at everyone, stretching out his little hands."[123] At the elevation of the Host and chalice following the Consecration, she saw the infant Jesus looking up to heaven and down at the congregation. This vision of the infant Jesus was repeated at Mass on the following two days.

The following year, Saint Faustina once again had a vision during the Christmas Midnight Mass of the infant Jesus reaching out to her. After Communion, the Lord said to her, **"I am always in your heart; not only when you receive me in Holy Communion, but always."**[124] At the Christmas Mass During the Night in 1936 Saint Faustina recorded in her diary how she experienced the presence of God in a way that pierced her entire being. Just before the elevation she saw a vision of the Holy Family. This was followed by a locution from the Blessed Virgin Mary: *"My daughter, Faustina, take this most precious Treasure."*[125] She then gave Faustina the infant Jesus, giving her indescribable joy. Suddenly, though, this vision was transformed into a vision of the suffering Christ. Following Communion, Faustina again experienced a deep sense of God's presence. Saint Faustina's experiences illustrate the teaching of Pope Pius XII that the Mass makes present all of the mysteries of Jesus' life. Even more, they show how "the Eucharist is a real and universal prolongation and extension of the mystery of the Incarnation."[126]

Special graces continued to be given to Faustina throughout the Christmas season. We will look at just one example. During the Mass of the Feast of Epiphany on January 6, 1937, Faustina described being "absorbed in the infinite majesty of

God." This experience was accompanied by an awareness "of how much God abases himself for my sake." Amazement and awe at this moving grace remained with her for the rest of the day. This experience inspired Faustina to pray for the world: "Taking advantage of the intimacy to which the Lord was admitting me, I interceded before him for the whole world. At such moments I have the feeling that the whole world is depending on me."[127]

Nurturing Eucharistic Amazement

There are many ways during Advent and Christmas to dispose oneself to receive the graces of these liturgical seasons. The suggested resources in this chapter can be easily found online or in print.

- Like Saint Faustina, make the practice of silence a part of every day. You can extend the practice of silence for any length of time, but if this is a new practice for you, you might find it helpful to begin with a short period, perhaps by a home altar or prayer corner. The *Catechism* recommends saying the name "Jesus" from time to time since he dwells within each person and invites you to abide in his love (see CCC 2666–2668; Jn 15:9).

- Add to your home altar an Advent wreath, a manger scene, and images of the infant Jesus and the Holy Family.

✦ Use images of the Immaculate Conception (December 8) and Our Lady of Guadalupe (December 12), the novena of the Immaculate Conception, as well as the Marian antiphon *Alma Redemptoris Mater* (Loving Mother of the Redeemer) to reflect on the Marian dimension of Advent and Christmas.

✦ Infuse all of your life with the spirit of Eucharistic amazement by volunteering at ministries that reflect an aspect of the liturgical season, such as the sacredness of life, the spirituality of giving, solidarity with those in need, simplicity, and peace in areas of conflict.

Lent

In the seasons of Lent and Easter, the Church commemorates liturgically Christ's paschal mystery—his work of redemption accomplished by his suffering, death, and resurrection, and ascension. Lent was a particularly important season for Faustina. On Ash Wednesday of 1937, Saint Faustina experienced the hidden stigmata during Mass. She writes in her diary, "I felt for a short time the passion of Jesus in my members."[128] During Lent she experienced a special concern for priests: "Lent is a very special time for the work of priests. We should assist them in rescuing souls."[129] Her Lenten disciplines that year, limited by her declining health, included sleeping without a pillow, fasting, and praying the Chaplet with her arms outstretched. Her intention for Lent was "to beg divine mercy for poor sinners, and for priests, the power to bring sinful hearts to repentance."[130] The following year, her last on earth, she began "in the way that Jesus wanted me to, making myself totally dependent upon his holy will and accepting with love everything that he sends me."[131] For Faustina, this included the will of God as it was communicated to her through her superior and her confessor, as well as God's instructions to her for promoting devotion to the Divine Mercy, interior inspirations for praying and making sacrifices for others, and ultimately whatever God might ask of her.

Holy Week was marked by an intimate participation in the final events of Christ's earthly life. On Palm Sunday 1936, the beginning of Holy Week, Faustina received insight into both the compassionate heart of Jesus and the anticipation of his passion. "I experienced in a special way," she wrote, "the sentiments of the most sweet Heart of Jesus." In spirit she saw his entrance upon a donkey's foal; the disciples with a crowd joyfully accompanying him with branches were met by a second crowd, including children, greeting him with branches and joyful cries. "But Jesus was very grave, and the Lord gave me to know how much he was suffering at the time. And at that moment, I saw nothing but only Jesus, whose Heart was saturated with ingratitude."[132] The following year she experienced Jesus' bitter suffering, and he shared with her "how much he had suffered in that triumphal procession. 'Hosanna' was reverberating in Jesus' heart as an echo of 'Crucify.' Jesus allowed me to feel this in a special way."[133] In the liturgical celebration Saint Faustina experienced the joy of Jesus' welcome, but also the suffering that would quickly follow.

Faustina left several accounts of her experiences during the Paschal Triduum—the three most solemn days of the liturgical year: Holy Thursday, Good Friday, and Easter. At the Holy Thursday Mass, which commemorates the night that Jesus instituted the Eucharist and the priesthood, washed the feet of his disciples, and was betrayed in the Garden of Gethsemane, Saint Faustina experienced visions, locutions, and a participation in Christ's passion. In 1935 she wrote that "when the moment for Holy Communion came, I saw the suffering Face of Jesus in every Host."[134] Two years later, she had a vision of the Lord and heard him say, "**Lean your head on my breast and rest.** The Lord pressed me to his Heart and said, **I shall give you a small portion of my passion, but do not be afraid, be brave; do not seek relief, but accept everything with submission to my will.**"[135] At his departure, she experienced intense spiritual pain. The next year, just months before her death, the Lord again appeared to her and said, "**Look into my Heart and see there the love and mercy which I have for mankind, and especially for sinners. Look, and enter into my passion.**" Her experience upon hearing those words was profound: "In an instant, I experienced and lived through the whole passion of Jesus in my own heart. I was surprised that these tortures did not deprive me of my life."[136] However, this was only the beginning of her participation in Christ's passion.

On Good Friday Saint Faustina received visions of Christ's passion as well as experiences of both his sufferings and his immense mercy, and a desire for the salvation of sinners. In

1936 she saw a vision of Christ on the cross: "At three o'clock, I saw the Lord Jesus crucified, who looked at me and said, **I thirst.** Then I saw two rays issue from his side, just as they appear in the image. I then felt in my soul the desire to save souls and to empty myself for the sake of poor sinners."[137] In 1937 she experienced the interior stigmata: "In the morning, I at once felt the torture of his five wounds in my body. This suffering continued until three o'clock. Although there is no outward sign of it, the torture is no less painful."[138] In 1938 she wrote, "I saw the Lord Jesus, tortured, but not nailed to the cross. It was still before the crucifixion, and he said to me, **You are my Heart. Speak to sinners about my mercy.** And the Lord gave me interior knowledge of the whole abyss of his mercy for souls."[139]

Nurturing Eucharistic Amazement

Lent for Saint Faustina was a time to unite herself with Christ in his sufferings.

- ❖ Set aside time to meditate on Christ's suffering. Pray the Way of the Cross (celebrated in many parishes on Fridays in Lent) and prayerfully read the passion narratives (see Mt 26:30–27:66; Mk 14:26–15:47; Lk 22:39–23:56; Jn 18:1–19:42).

- ❖ Since the seventh century the Church has prayed the seven penitential psalms particularly during Lent. You can enter into the suffering of Christ by praying these: Psalms 6, 32, 38, 51, 102, 130, and 143.

✦ Unite yourself to Mary by praying the Lenten Marian prayers: the Seven Sorrows of Mary and the *Ave Regina Caelorum* (Hail, Queen of Heaven).

✦ Additions to a home altar could include the image of the Divine Mercy and a palm from Palm Sunday.

Easter Season

Just as Saint Faustina shared in the Lord's suffering and abandonment during Lent, so she shared in the joy and power of his resurrection. In 1937 at the Easter Sunday Mass During the Day, she received a vision and locution of the risen Lord. "I saw the Lord in beauty and splendor, and he said to me, **My daughter, peace be with you. . . .** My heart was fortified for struggle and sufferings."[140] The following year during Mass she expressed her profound gratitude to the Lord for redeeming us and "for having given us that greatest of all gifts; namely, his love in Holy Communion; that is, his very own Self. At that moment, I was drawn into the bosom of the Most Holy Trinity, and I was immersed in the love of the Father, the Son and the Holy Spirit."[141]

In 1935, the Sunday following Easter, the Feast of Divine Mercy, was especially significant for the Apostle of Mercy.[142] As the priest was giving the benediction (blessing) with the

Blessed Sacrament at the end of the service, Saint Faustina saw the Lord as he appeared in the Divine Mercy image. "The Lord gave his blessing, and the rays extended over the whole world." This was followed by a vision representing the Trinity. It began with a dwelling place of crystal bathed in light that could not be penetrated. Faustina then saw three doors leading to it, and then Jesus, as he appeared in the Divine Mercy image, "entered this resplendence through the second door to the Unity within. It is a triple Unity, which is incomprehensible—which is infinity." Jesus then explained the meaning of this vision: **"This Feast emerged from the very depths of my mercy, and it is confirmed in the vast depths of my tender mercies. Every soul believing and trusting in my mercy will obtain it."** Saint Faustina rejoiced at the majesty and goodness of God.[143]

Two years later, in 1937, Saint Faustina had a similar experience of the Trinity on this same Feast after Communion: "I was united to the Three Divine Persons in such a way that when I was united to Jesus, I was simultaneously united to the Father and the Holy Spirit." She rejoiced at the experience of God's infinite mercy, and the experience gave her a deep longing that "souls would want to understand how much God loves them!"[144]

On the Ascension of Our Lord that same year, 1937, she again experienced communion with the Trinity. She writes that, following Holy Communion, "my soul was drawn into the glowing center of love. I understood that no exterior works could stand comparison with pure love of God . . . I saw the joy of the Incarnate Word, and I was immersed in the Divine Trinity." When she returned to her senses she wrote, "I call this day an uninterrupted ecstasy of love. The whole universe seemed to me like a tiny drop in comparison with God."[145]

Nurturing Eucharistic Amazement

For Saint Faustina the Easter season was imbued with the joy, mercy, and love of the Trinity, blessings that we too can foster.

- Cultivate the graces of Easter by praying the Chaplet of the Divine Mercy and the Pentecost novena.

- Consider having your home blessed with Easter water, a cherished tradition.

- Pray the Marian antiphon for the Easter season, the *Regina Caeli* (Hail, Queen of Heaven).

- Use for meditation the *Via Lucis* (the Way of Light), encouraged by the Church during the Easter season. Using the Way of the Cross as a model, the *Via Lucis* helps us contemplate Jesus' appearances from the resurrection to the ascension.

- The Trinity was an important Easter theme for Saint Faustina. Consider using 2 Corinthians 13:13, which is Saint Paul's Trinitarian blessing, for personal meditation or as a family blessing.

A Deeper Knowledge of God

Faustina believed that the feasts of the Church gave her "a deeper knowledge of God and a special grace."[146] In addition to the major liturgical seasons that we have considered, she confided to her diary the graces she received on many of the major feasts of the liturgical year. The Solemnity of the Immaculate Conception, which falls during Advent on December 8, was an important feast for Faustina. In 1935 she wrote:

> During Holy Mass, I heard the rustling of garments and saw the most holy Mother of God in a most beautiful radiance. Her white garment was girdled with a blue sash. She said to me, *You give me great joy when you adore the Holy Trinity for the graces and privileges which were accorded me.* And she immediately disappeared.[147]

Two years later, before Communion on this solemnity, the Blessed Virgin Mary urged Saint Faustina to

> *practice the three virtues that are dearest to me—and most pleasing to God. The first is humility, humility, and once again humility; the second virtue, purity; the third virtue, love of God. As my daughter, you must especially radiate with these virtues.*

Faustina was obedient to the Virgin's words, writing that "They are as though engraved in my heart."[148]

The Trinity and Sacred Heart of Jesus were also significant celebrations for Faustina. On one occasion she received a locution after Communion: "**You are Our dwelling place.** At that moment, I felt in my soul the presence of the Holy

Trinity, the Father, the Son, and the Holy Spirit. I felt that I was the temple of God. I felt I was a child of the Father."[149] On the Solemnity of the Holy Trinity 1937, she experienced union with the Trinity during Mass. "I was united to the Three Persons. And once I was united to One of these Most Venerable Persons, I was, at the same time, united to the other Two Persons."[150] The fruit again was great joy, but also a sadness at her inability to put her experience into words.

Two weeks later, on the Feast of the Sacred Heart, the Lord gave her during Mass "the knowledge of the Heart of Jesus and of the nature of the fire of love with which he burns for us and of how he is an Ocean of Mercy." She then heard a voice: "**Apostle of my mercy, proclaim to the whole world my unfathomable mercy. Do not be discouraged by the difficulties you encounter in proclaiming my mercy.**"[151] He explained that the difficulties were necessary for two reasons: Faustina's sanctification and as proof that this was God's work. The Lord then instructed her to write down all that God told her about his mercy, because it would profit many souls.

Faustina left two accounts of the concluding feast of the liturgical year, the Feast of Christ the King, October 27, 1935 and October 25, 1936. During Mass in 1935 she prayed that Jesus would rule in all hearts and grace would illumine every soul. She then heard him say, "**My daughter, you give me the greatest glory by faithfully fulfilling my desires.**"[152] The following year, during Mass she wrote, "I was so enveloped in the great interior fire of God's love and the desire to save souls that I do not know how to express it. I feel I am all aflame. I shall fight all evil with the weapon of mercy. I am being burned up by the desire to save souls."[153]

First Fridays

In addition to the seasons and feasts of the liturgical year, Faustina often received special graces on First Fridays.[154] During Mass on the First Friday of September 1937 she wrote in her diary, "Jesus gave me to know that even the smallest thing does not happen on earth without his will. . . . God can deal with me as he pleases, and I will bless him for everything."[155] This left her with a great peace, especially about her mission to spread the message of Divine Mercy. On another First Friday she wrote:

> This morning during Mass, for a brief while, I saw the suffering Savior. What struck me was that Jesus was so peaceful amidst his great sufferings. I understood that this was a lesson for me on what my outward behavior should be in the midst of my various sufferings.[156]

On the First Friday during Lent of 1936 after Communion, she had a vision in which a hand gave her a ciborium filled with sacred hosts and a voice said, **"These are hosts which have been received by the souls for whom you have obtained the grace of true conversion during this Lent."**[157] On the First Friday of October 1936, Jesus spoke to her after Communion: **"Now I know that it is not for the graces or gifts that you love me, but because my will is dearer to you than life. That is why I am uniting myself with you so intimately as with no other creature."**[158]

Nurturing Eucharistic Amazement

The celebration of the feasts and Nine First Fridays suggests a number of devotions that reflect the different aspects of Jesus' life and public ministry.

- In your prayer, incorporate devotions such as the Litany of the Sacred Heart and the Litany of the Holy Name of Jesus. These litanies present various aspects of the person and work of our Redeemer for prayer and meditation and can be prayed individually or collectively, at home or before the Blessed Sacrament.

- Increase your devotion to Mary through the Rosary and other Marian devotions, including the antiphon *Salve, Regina* (Hail, Holy Queen) and the Litany of the Blessed Virgin Mary, also known as the Litany of Loreto.

- Your encounter with Jesus in the Mass will be enriched by spending time with him in Eucharistic Adoration, which prepares you in a particular way to receive the graces of Mass and extends your praise and worship.

- In the season of Ordinary Time, add to your home altar liturgically appropriate additions such as images or icons from Jesus' public ministry, including, for example, the wedding at Cana, the prodigal son, or Jesus' miracles.

✦ If the First Friday devotion is new to you, consider learning more about this devotion and making it part of your spiritual life.

Hands Full of Graces

On several occasions the Lord explained to Faustina how he wanted us to welcome him in Communion. During one Mass the Lord showed her how important it was to receive him with great faith. Jesus said to her, "**I am the same under each of the species, but not every soul receives me with the same living faith as you do, my daughter, and therefore I cannot act in their souls as I do in yours.**"[159] On another occasion he told her, "**For me to be able to act upon a soul, the soul must have faith. O how pleasing to me is living faith!**"[160]

The Lord also explained to Faustina the importance of concentrating one's attention on him after Communion:

> When I come to a human heart in Holy Communion, my hands are full of all kinds of graces which I want to give to the soul. But souls do not even pay any attention to Me; they leave me to myself and busy themselves with other things. Oh, how sad I am that souls do not recognize Love! They treat me as a dead object.[161]

Those who do not perceive by faith the living Person beneath the appearances of bread and wine do not experience the blessings he has for them.

> **I wait for souls, and they are indifferent toward Me. I love them tenderly and sincerely, and they distrust Me. I want to lavish my graces on them, and they do not want to accept them. They treat me as a dead object, whereas my heart is full of love and mercy.**[162]

Faustina is a compelling witness that Christ comes to us in the Eucharist with great love and mercy, ready to lavish upon us his richest graces.

It is worth noting here the similarity between these passages from Faustina's *Diary* and the teaching of Saint Teresa of Avila. The Lord spoke to Faustina about the importance of receiving him with living faith, and Teresa wrote of the importance of approaching the Eucharist with both faith and love. Jesus told Faustina of his desire to lavish graces on us, and Teresa said that receiving the Eucharist just once with great faith and love would fill us with blessings. Both saints lament those who receive the Lord and immediately turn their thoughts to worldly matters. The Lord assured Faustina of his living presence beneath the appearances of bread and wine. Similarly, Teresa reminded her nuns that after Communion Jesus himself was with them. Both saints approached Communion with great faith and love, and both experienced the love and mercy of the Lord in the Eucharist.

Nurturing Eucharistic Amazement

Three exhortations appear often in Saint Faustina's experiences: invoke God's mercy, pray for others, and do God's will. The Mass includes all three, and one can add a silent petition at these moments:

- At the beginning of Mass God's mercy is implored in the *Kyrie* (Lord, have mercy) and in the Gloria, and again before Communion in the Lamb of God.

- The Eucharistic Prayers include intercessions for all members of the Church, living and dead, and for the peace and salvation of the whole world.

- Pope Benedict XVI says that the Presentation of the Gifts at the start of the Liturgy of the Eucharist is also a form of intercession—in addition to the bread and wine, you can also bring to God all of the sorrow and anguish of the world.

- Before Communion ask God to grant the Church peace and unity according to his will, and in the Our Father ask that his will be done.

Our liturgical prayer can inform our personal prayer, and our devotional prayer can deepen our participation in liturgical prayer.

Conclusion

Faustina's experiences throughout the liturgical year indicate the blessings available to us when we live the liturgical year fully. The graces she received during Advent and Christmas included visions of the infant Jesus and the Holy Family, joy, and insights into Christ's condescension as well as his majesty, power, and love. Lent and Easter offer a striking contrast. During Lent she received visions and experiences of Jesus' suffering, including the hidden stigmata. The season of Easter brought locutions from Christ and his Blessed Mother, a deep sense of gratitude, and experiences of the Trinity. Feast days made present different graces, especially Trinity Sunday, the Sacred Heart of Jesus, the Immaculate Conception of the Blessed Virgin Mary, and the Solemnity of Our Lord Jesus Christ, King of the Universe. Inspired by the example of Saint Faustina, we will turn now to consider ways in which we ourselves can prepare for Mass and be better disposed to receive the unique graces of each celebration.

Notes

115. Bernard of Clairvaux, *Love Without Measure: Extracts from the Writings of Saint Bernard of Clairvaux*, introduced and arranged by Paul Diemer OSCO (Kalamazoo: Cistercian Publications, 1990), 69.

116. Silvano Giordano, *God Speaks in the Night: The Life, Times, and Teaching of Saint John of the Cross*, trans. Kieran Kavanaugh, OCD (Washington, DC: ICS Publications, 2000), 207.

117. Thérèse of Lisieux, *Story of a Soul: The Autobiography of St. Thérèse of Lisieux*, 41.

118. John Paul II, "Homily for the Mass in St. Peter's Square for the Canonization of Sr. Mary Faustina Kowalska," April 30, 2000, The Holy See, Vatican.va. https://www.vatican.va/content/john-paul-ii/en/homilies/2000/documents/hf_jp-ii_hom_20000430_faustina.html.

119. Maria Faustina Kowalska, *Diary of Saint Maria Faustina Kowalska: Divine Mercy in My Soul* (Stockbridge: Marian Press, 2012), para. 6.

120. Kowalska, *Diary of St. Faustina*, para. 895. We will follow the style of the *Diary*, indicating the words of Christ in boldface and the words of the Blessed Virgin Mary in italics.

121. Kowalska, *Diary of St. Faustina*, para. 1398.

122. Kowalska, *Diary of St. Faustina*, para. 1437.

123. Kowalska, *Diary of St. Faustina*, para. 347. Before the Prayer over the Offerings the priest offers the host and wine, unconsecrated at this point, accompanied by prayers that anticipate their transubstantiation into the Body and Blood of Christ.

124. Kowalska, *Diary of St. Faustina*, para. 575.

125. Kowalska, *Diary of St. Faustina*, para. 846. A locution is an experience of receiving internally a communication from God, often during prayer.

126. Matthias Joseph Scheeben, *The Mysteries of Christianity* (New York: The Crossroads Publishing Company), 485.

127. Kowalska, *Diary of St. Faustina*, para. 870.

128. Kowalska, *Diary of St. Faustina*, para. 931.

129. Kowalska, *Diary of St. Faustina*, para. 931.

130. Kowalska, *Diary of St. Faustina*, para. 934.

131. Kowalska, *Diary of St. Faustina*, para. 1625.

132. Kowalska, *Diary of St. Faustina*, para. 642.

133. Kowalska, *Diary of St. Faustina*, para. 1028.

134. Kowalska, *Diary of St. Faustina*, para. 413.

135. Kowalska, *Diary of St. Faustina*, para. 1053.

136. Kowalska, *Diary of St. Faustina*, para. 1663.

137. Kowalska, *Diary of St. Faustina*, para. 648.

138. Kowalska, *Diary of St. Faustina*, para. 1055.

139. Kowalska, *Diary of St. Faustina*, para. 1666.

140. Kowalska, *Diary of St. Faustina*, para. 1067.

141. Kowalska, *Diary of St. Faustina*, para. 1670.

142. Faustina is referring here to a locution she received in 1931 regarding the Feast of Mercy, which was to be celebrated on the Second Sunday of Easter (*Diary of St. Faustina*, para. 49). Saint John Paul II added this feast to the General Roman Calendar in 2000.

143. Kowalska, *Diary of St. Faustina*, para. 420.

144. Kowalska, *Diary of St. Faustina*, para. 1073.

145. Kowalska, *Diary of St. Faustina*, para. 1121.

146. Kowalska, *Diary of St. Faustina*, para. 481.

147. Kowalska, *Diary of St. Faustina*, para. 564.

148. Kowalska, *Diary of St. Faustina*, para. 1415.

149. Kowalska, *Diary of St. Faustina*, para. 451.

152. Kowalska, *Diary of St. Faustina*, para. 1129.

151. Kowalska, *Diary of St. Faustina*, para. 1142.

152. Kowalska, *Diary of St. Faustina*, para. 500.

153. Kowalska, *Diary of St. Faustina*, para. 745.

154. This is a reference to the promise given to Saint Margaret Mary Alacoque (†1690) of the grace of final penitence to those who receive communion on the First Friday in nine consecutive months. Congregation for Divine Worship, *Directory on Popular Piety and the Liturgy*, December 2001, The Holy See, Vatican.va, 171. https://www.vatican.va/roman_curia/congregations/ccdds/documentsrc_con_ccdds_doc_20020513_vers–direttorio_en.html.

155. Kowalska, *Diary of St. Faustina*, para. 1262.

156. Kowalska, *Diary of St. Faustina*, para. 1467.

157. Kowalska, *Diary of St. Faustina*, para. 640.

158. Kowalska, *Diary of St. Faustina*, para. 707.

159. Kowalska, *Diary of St. Faustina*, para. 1407.

160. Kowalska, *Diary of St. Faustina*, para. 1420.

161. Kowalska, *Diary of St. Faustina*, para. 1385.

162. Kowalska, *Diary of St. Faustina*, para. 1447.

CHAPTER 7

Preparing for Mass

I prepare myself for each feast and unite myself closely to
the spirit of the Church.

DIARY OF SAINT MARIA FAUSTINA KOWALSKA

IN ANTICIPATION OF THE Feast of the Immaculate
Conception in 1937 Saint Faustina wrote, "It is with great
zeal that I have prepared for the celebration of the Feast of the
Immaculate Conception of the Mother of God. I have made
an extra effort to keep recollected in spirit and have meditated on the unique privilege of Our Lady."[163] Although Saint
Faustina experienced many unexpected graces during Mass,
excerpts from her *Diary* reveal that she regularly prepared
herself for upcoming liturgical seasons and feasts. This preparation was vital to deepening her union with the Church, the
mystical Body of Christ, Head and members, for the glory of
God and for the salvation of souls.

The detailed commentaries on the liturgical year written by Prosper Guéranger and Pius Parsch were designed to help the faithful enter into the unique graces of each liturgical season and celebration. Their works, along with the example of Saint Faustina, suggest ways a person can prepare to receive the unique graces offered in each of the seasons and feasts of the liturgical year. In this chapter we will follow the method of Guéranger, Parsch, and others as we reflect on the parts of each Mass that vary from season to season, from feast to feast, and from week to week: the entrance and Communion antiphons, biblical readings, prayers, and prefaces. Prayerful attention to the liturgy can suggest to us the graces of each celebration. Below is an outline of the parts of the Sunday Mass—the words in bold italics are the variable parts at which we will look more closely.

THE INTRODUCTORY RITES

Entrance Antiphon

Greeting

Penitential Act

Kyrie

Gloria

Collect

THE LITURGY OF THE WORD

First Reading

Responsorial Psalm

Second Reading

Gospel Acclamation

Gospel Reading

Homily

Profession of Faith

Prayer of the Faithful

THE LITURGY OF THE EUCHARIST

Presentation and Preparation of the Gifts

   Offertory Chant

Prayer over the Offerings

The Eucharistic Prayer

   Preface

   The Eucharistic Prayers

The Communion Rite

   The Lord's Prayer

   Rite of Peace

   Lamb of God

   Invitation to Communion

   Communion

   Communion Antiphon

Prayer after Communion

THE CONCLUDING RITES

[Announcements]

Final Blessing

Dismissal

Entrance Antiphon

The first indication of the specific graces made present in a given Mass is found in the *entrance antiphon*, usually just one sentence from Sacred Scripture that introduces "the mystery of the liturgical time or festivity."[164] A good example is the familiar entrance antiphon for the Third Sunday of Advent from Philippians 4:4, 5: "Rejoice in the Lord always; again I will say, Rejoice. The Lord is near."[165] This verse announces the theme of joy that characterizes this Sunday, known as Gaudete Sunday from the Latin word for "rejoice"—*Gaudete*. On this Sunday the Church also signals the theme of joy by the option for the priest to use rose vestments as a visual sign of the Church's exhortation for us to rejoice, an example of how the liturgy appeals to our different senses.

The entrance antiphon for the memorial of Saint Thérèse of Lisieux (October 1) weaves together a scripture of great importance to the saint with excerpts from her writings. It is a good example of the theological and spiritual richness of the entrance antiphon:

> The Lord led her and taught her,
> and kept her as the apple of his eye.
> Like an eagle spreading its wings
> he took her up and bore her on his shoulders.
> The Lord alone was her guide.[166]

The biblical source for this antiphon is Deuteronomy 32:11–12: "As an eagle stirs up its nest, and hovers over its young; as it spreads its wings, takes them up, and bears them aloft on its pinions, the LORD alone guided him." Both the reference to the Lord as the sole guide and the metaphor of the eagle are found also in Thérèse's diary. A few months after she entered the cloister, a priest told her, "My child, may our Lord always be your Superior and your Novice Master," after which Thérèse referred several times to Jesus as "my Director."[167] Thérèse also referred to herself as Jesus' "little bird" in contrast to "the angels and saints who rise like eagles before the consuming Fire"[168]—God. "My *folly* consists in begging the eagles, my brothers, to obtain for me the favor of flying toward the Sun of Love with the *Divine Eagle's own wings!*"[169] This antiphon combines a key passage from the Bible with words and images from the saint's own writings to convey the essence of her spirituality, which has been such a powerful gift to the Church.

These examples illustrate how the entrance antiphon for each Mass concisely expresses the theme of the celebration by recalling its Old Testament types, encapsulating its meaning in a key verse, or summarizing its spirituality.

Collect

The next variable part of the Mass is the Opening Prayer, which expresses "the character of the celebration."[170] It is known as the *Collect* because it "collects" or "gathers up, as it were, all the petitions that the faithful have expressed privately."[171] Along with the entrance antiphon, it too indicates the special graces of the celebration. Consider a few examples. The Collect for Pentecost, the outpouring of the Holy Spirit on the first disciples, asks that the splendor of God's "glory may shine forth upon us / and that, by the bright rays of the Holy Spirit, / the light of your light may confirm the hearts / of those born again by your grace."[172] The Collect for the Immaculate Conception of the Blessed Virgin Mary requests that "through her intercession, / we, too, may be cleansed and admitted to your presence."[173] The Collect for the Sixth Sunday in Ordinary Time recalls that God abides "in hearts that are just and true" and asks "that we may be so fashioned by your grace / as to become a dwelling pleasing to you."[174] The Collect for the Memorial of Saint Francis of Assisi on October 4 asks God that we, walking like Saint Francis in "poverty and humility / . . . may follow your Son, / and, through joyful charity, / come to be united with you."[175] The Collect expresses some of the graces that God is making present in each Mass.

Readings

The *scriptural readings* are the next variable part of the Mass, and they offer further indications of the specific graces of each liturgical celebration, for "when the Sacred Scriptures are read in the Church, God himself speaks to his people."[176] Over the course of the liturgical year, the readings at Mass "unfold the whole mystery of Christ, from the incarnation and birth until the ascension, the day of Pentecost, and the expectation of the blessed hope and of the coming of the Lord" (SC 102). The readings for Sunday Mass typically begin with a reading from the Old Testament and a responsorial psalm, followed by a passage from one of the New Testament epistles and the Gospel. The Gospel is the culmination of the Liturgy of the Word, and the Old Testament passage and responsorial psalm prefigure or illumine it in some way. This arrangement "helps us to understand the unity of God's plan thanks to the interplay of the Old and New Testament readings" (VD 57) whose center is the person and work of Christ. Thus, when the Church proclaims the Word of God from the Old and New Testaments, she "is proclaiming one and the same mystery of Christ . . . the center and fullness of the whole of Scripture."[177] The readings for each Mass proclaim "the principal deeds and words belonging to the history of salvation" in order to make clear to us "that the history of salvation is continued here and now in the representation of Christ's paschal mystery celebrated through the Eucharist."[178]

Prayer over the Offerings

The next variable element is the *Prayer over the Offerings*, which is introduced by the priest's invitation to the people to pray "that my sacrifice and yours may be acceptable to God, the almighty Father."[179] The prayer that follows often includes a petition for a fruitful reception of the Eucharist. For example, the Prayer over the Offerings for the Feast of Our Lady of Guadalupe on December 12 asks God to "grant that this sacrifice / may strengthen us to fulfill your commandments / as true children of the Virgin Mary."[180] On Palm

Sunday we ask that "we may feel already the effects of your mercy,"[181] and at the Christmas Vigil Mass we ask the Lord that we may "serve you all the more eagerly."[182] The prayers during Ordinary Time include petitions for unity—that "by partaking of the sacred mystery, / we may be faithfully united in mind and heart"[183]—and for charity—"lead us to grow in charity."[184] The Prayer over the Offerings gives voice to the needs and desires of our heart throughout the liturgical year.

Preface

The Prayer over the Offerings leads directly into the *Preface*, the beginning of the Eucharistic Prayer. It is introduced by the dialogue between the priest and the people. The Church has provided nearly a hundred Prefaces for use throughout the liturgical year. Some are specific to a particular feast, such as the Transfiguration or the Assumption. Others are used during the different liturgical seasons, such as Lent, Easter, or Ordinary Time, or on the feasts of saints. The Preface is always a prayer to the Father that offers a concise summary of the theology and graces of the celebration.

One of the Prefaces for Advent invites us to be "watchful in prayer and exultant in his praise."[185] Christmas, "the mystery of the Word made flesh," is the time when the light of God's glory "has shone upon the eyes of our mind," so that we can recognize in Christ "God made visible" and "be caught up through him in love of things invisible."[186] Lent is "a sacred time for the renewing and purifying" of our hearts so that, "freed from disordered affections," we can use "the things of this passing world" in such a way as "to hold rather to the things that eternally endure."[187] The Easter season makes present the power of the paschal mystery through which "a universe cast down is renewed, / and integrity of life is restored to us in Christ."[188]

On the last Sunday of the liturgical year, the Solemnity of Our Lord Jesus, King of the Universe, we participate in Christ's work of offering to the Father "a kingdom of truth and life, / a kingdom of holiness and grace, / a kingdom of justice, love and peace."[189] Preface I of Saints proclaims: "By their way of life you offer us an example, / by communion with them you give us companionship, / by their intercession, sure support, / so that . . . / we may run as victors in the race before us."[190] The Prefaces teach us about the unique graces of both seasons and individual feasts. They are rich and beautiful prayers that amply repay prayerful reflection and study.

Prayer after Communion

The final variable part of the Mass is the *Prayer after Communion*. This prayer, which concludes the Communion Rite and completes the prayer of the assembly, "prays for the fruits of the mystery just celebrated,"[191] its special— peculiar—graces. The Prayer after Communion for the Most Sacred Heart of Jesus asks for an increase of love and charity: "May this sacrament of charity, O Lord, / make us fervent with the fire of holy love, / so that, drawn always to your Son, / we may learn to see him in our neighbor."[192] The prayer for the Christmas Vigil requests "that we may draw new vigor /

from celebrating the Nativity of your Only Begotten Son, /
by whose heavenly mystery we receive both food and
drink."[193] The Ash Wednesday prayer is a petition that the
Eucharist we have just received may "sustain us, O Lord, /
that our Lenten fast may be pleasing to you / and be for us a
healing remedy."[194] Each petition for grace expresses the
character of the celebration.

Gift and Responsibility

Throughout the liturgical year the Church "opens up to the
faithful the riches of her Lord's powers and merits, so that these
are in some way made present for all time, and the faithful are
enabled to lay hold upon them and become filled with saving
grace" (SC 102). But this gift implies a responsibility on our
part. In the words of Pope Pius XII, "It requires a diligent and
well-ordered study on our part to be able to know and praise
our Redeemer ever more and more" (MD 161). This preparation is not something we do on our own—it is something that
we, ministers and assembly, do with the guidance of the Holy
Spirit. The Holy Spirit accomplishes what we cannot, preparing us to receive the blessings of each Mass—through faith,
through an openness to conversion, and through a desire to do
the Father's will—which transform our lives. When we
approach, prepare, and celebrate the liturgical year in this way,
it becomes "a splendid hymn of praise offered to the heavenly
Father by the Christian family through Jesus, their perpetual
Mediator" (MD 161).

Divine Reading—*Lectio Divina*

Reflecting on the prayers and readings of the Mass can be a fruitful preparation for receiving the graces of each Eucharistic celebration. Saint John Chrysostom encouraged his flock to prepare for Mass by meditating on the Sunday Gospel. He suggested that they read the passage several times, reflect on it, study it, and analyze it. In this way, he told them, "your minds will be already made familiar with the sense of the words, and you will become keener and more clear-sighted not for hearing only, nor for learning, but also for the teaching of others."[195]

John Chrysostom's instructions are an example of the ancient practice of *lectio divina*, a Latin phrase that means "divine reading," a method originally developed by the early monks as a fruitful way to read the Sacred Scriptures. In the twelfth century, a monk named Guigo II (†1188) wrote the classic description of *lectio divina* in a short treatise entitled *The Ladder of Monks*, one of the most widely praised and read works of its kind.

One day while engaged in manual labor, Guigo was thinking about spiritual exercise. He described how "all at once four stages in spiritual exercise came into my mind: reading, meditation, prayer and contemplation." These four stages formed a ladder (hence the title) that lifts us "from earth to heaven. It has few rungs, yet its length is immense and wonderful, for its lower end rests upon the earth, but its top pierces the clouds and touches heavenly secrets."[196] The four rungs of this ladder—reading, meditation, prayer, and contemplation—are interconnected, each one leading on to the next. Medieval monks like Guigo considered them to be four "phases of a single movement involving the mind, the heart, the will, and the body."[197]

In *The Ladder of Monks*, Guigo explained each stage and emphasized their interconnectedness. *Reading*, the first stage, is the "foundation," he said, since "it provides the subject matter we must use for meditation."[198] It carefully and attentively listens to the text, "concentrating all one's powers on it." *Meditation* is more analytical, seeking "with the help of one's own reason for knowledge of hidden truth."[199] It "goes to the heart of the matter, examines each point thoroughly."[200] Meditation in turn "directs us to prayer. *Prayer* lifts itself up to God with all its strength, and begs for the treasure it longs for, which is the sweetness of contemplation."[201] It is "the heart's devoted turning to God to drive away evil and obtain what is good."[202] In the final stage, *contemplation*, we rest in the presence of God and are "in some sort lifted up to God," tasting "the joys of everlasting sweetness."[203] In summary, wrote Guigo, "Reading works on the outside, meditation on the pith: prayer asks for what we long for, contemplation gives us delight in the sweetness we have found."[204] The goal of divine reading is not an intellectual mastery of Scripture but friendship with God; it is holiness: "Reading seeks for the sweetness of a blessed life, meditation perceives it, prayer asks for it, contemplation tastes it."[205]

Guigo's method has been encouraged by recent popes. Saint John Paul II said that "listening to the word of God should become a life-giving encounter, in the ancient and ever valid tradition of *lectio divina*, which draws from the biblical text the living Word which questions, directs and shapes our lives."[206] Pope Benedict XVI wrote that *lectio divina* is "capable of opening up to the faithful the treasures of God's word, but also of bringing about an encounter with Christ, the living Word of God" (VD 87). Pope Francis described it as "one particular way of listening to what the Lord wishes to tell us in his word and of letting ourselves be transformed by the Spirit."[207] Although originally practiced with biblical passages, *lectio divina* can be used with the other texts of the Mass—the prayers, antiphons, the Preface, even the Eucharistic Prayer—and lead to an encounter with Christ and transformation by the Spirit.

Nurturing Eucharistic Amazement

For readers unfamiliar with *lectio divina*, what follows is an example using a passage from the Gospel of Mark that is proclaimed on the Sixteenth Sunday in Ordinary Time (Year B in the three-year cycle of Sunday readings). Choose a quiet location conducive to prayer, setting aside at least fifteen minutes, although this of course will vary. Here is the passage:

> The apostles gathered together with Jesus and reported all they had done and taught. He said to them, "Come away by yourselves to a deserted place and rest a while." People were coming and going in great numbers, and they had no opportunity even

to eat. So they went off in the boat by themselves to a deserted place. People saw them leaving and many came to know about it. They hastened there on foot from all the towns and arrived at the place before them.

When he disembarked and saw the vast crowd, his heart was moved with pity for them, for they were like sheep without a shepherd; and he began to teach them many things. (Mk 6:30–34)

Reading is the first step. Read through this passage several times, slowly and deliberately. Try reading it silently and aloud. In this step you are simply listening to the passage. *Meditating* is the second step. This is when you analyze and reflect on the text. What is happening? What is Jesus doing? Saying? Feeling? Who else is in this passage? What strikes you about the text? What puzzles you? In this passage, for example, you might notice Jesus' concern for the apostles, their need for rest, the crowd watching and following them, Jesus' compassion when he sees them, the description of abandoned sheep, their desire to hear from Jesus. Focus on one or two details that speak to you. Let this lead naturally to the third step, *praying*. What prayer does your reading and meditating suggest? It may be praise and thanksgiving for Jesus' compassion; a petition for rest, mercy, or knowledge; or intercession for those you know who are in need of a shepherd. This gradually becomes *contemplation*, the fourth step, resting in the presence of the compassionate Shepherd. Conclude by thanking God for his word and his presence.

Conclusion

The Church and her saints urge us to prepare ourselves to participate in the Mass. A deeper knowledge of the Mass and familiarity with the readings and prayers of each celebration (the Propers) can contribute to our fruitful participation in the Mass. The Propers for each Mass indicate the special graces of each celebration, and the ancient method of *lectio divina* is a proven method for prayerfully reflecting on these texts. In this way we, like Saint Faustina, can prepare ourselves for each celebration and unite ourselves "closely with the spirit of the Church."[208] Saint Teresa of Avila and Saint Faustina have enlightened and strengthened our faith and understanding of Christ's transforming action in the Mass. We will now explore the Eucharist with our third saint, Saint John Chrysostom, the Doctor of the Eucharist.

Notes

163. Kowalska, *Diary of St. Faustina*, para. 1412.

164. *General Instruction of the Roman Missal* (GIRM), para. 47.

165. *Roman Missal*, Third Sunday of Advent, Entrance antiphon.

166. *Roman Missal*, October 1, Saint Thérèse of the Child Jesus, Virgin and Doctor of the Church, Entrance antiphon.

167. Thérèse of Lisieux, *Story of a Soul*, 150.

168. Thérèse of Lisieux, *Story of a Soul*, 199.

169. Thérèse of Lisieux, *Story of a Soul*, 200.

170. *General Instruction of the Roman Missal* (GIRM), para. 54.

171. Robert Cabié, *The Eucharist*, trans. Matthew J. O'Connell, *The Church at Prayer, vol. 2* (Collegeville, MN: The Liturgical Press, 1986), 53.

172. *Roman Missal*, Pentecost, At the Vigil Mass, Collect.

173. *Roman Missal*, December 8, The Immaculate Conception of the Blessed Virgin Mary, Collect.

174. *Roman Missal*, Sixth Sunday in Ordinary Time, Collect.

175. *Roman Missal*, October 4, Saint Francis of Assisi, Collect.

176. *General Instruction of the Roman Missal* (GIRM), para. 29.

177. *Lectionary for Mass*, 5.

178. *Lectionary for Mass*, 61. To illustrate this, consider the readings for the Exaltation of the Holy Cross on September 14.

179. *Roman Missal*, Order of Mass 29.

180. *Roman Missal*, December 12, Our Lady of Guadalupe, Prayer over the Offerings.

181. *Roman Missal*, Palm Sunday of the Passion of the Lord, Prayer over the Offerings.

182. *Roman Missal*, The Nativity of the Lord [Christmas], At the Vigil Mass, Prayer over the Offerings.

183. *Roman Missal*, Twenty-Third Sunday in Ordinary Time, Prayer over the Offerings.

184. *Roman Missal*, Tenth Sunday in Ordinary Time, Prayer over the Offerings.

185. *Roman Missal*, Order of Mass (Preface II of Advent) 34.

186. *Roman Missal*, Order of Mass (Preface I of the Nativity of the Lord) 35.

187. *Roman Missal*, Order of Mass (Preface II of Lent) 40.

188. *Roman Missal*, Order of Mass (Preface IV of Easter) 48.

189. *Roman Missal*, Last Sunday in Ordinary Time, Our Lord Jesus Christ, King of the Universe (Preface: Christ, King of the Universe).

190. *Roman Missal*, Order of Mass (Preface I of Saints) 66.

191. *General Instruction of the Roman Missal* (GIRM), para. 89.

192. *Roman Missal*, The Most Sacred Heart of Jesus, Prayer after Communion.

193. *Roman Missal*, The Nativity of the Lord [Christmas], Prayer after Communion.

194. *Roman Missal*, Ash Wednesday, Prayer after Communion.

195. John Chrysostom, *Homilies on the Gospel of Saint John*, trans. Philip Schaff, NPNF 14 (Edinburgh: T&T Clark, 1993), 14, 11.1.38.

196. Edmund Colledge, OSA and James Walsh, SJ, eds., trans., *Guigo II: The Ladder of Monks: A Letter on the Contemplative Life and Twelve Meditations* (Kalamazoo: Cistercian Publications, 1979), 67–68.

197. Timothy Fry, OSB, ed., RB 1980: *The Rule of Saint Benedict in Latin and English with Notes* (Collegeville: The Liturgical Press, 1981), 447.

198. Colledge and Walsh, *Guigo II*, 79.

199. Colledge and Walsh, *Guigo II*, 68.

200. Colledge and Walsh, *Guigo II*, 70.

201. Colledge and Walsh, *Guigo II*, 79. Italics added.

202. Colledge and Walsh, *Guigo II*, 68.

203. Colledge and Walsh, *Guigo II*, 68.

204. Colledge and Walsh, *Guigo II*, 69.

205. Colledge and Walsh, *Guigo II*, 68–69.

206. John Paul II, *Novo Millennio Ineunte* (January 6, 2001), The Holy See, Vatican.va, 39. https://www.vatican.va/content/john-paul-ii/en/apost_letters/2001/documents/hf_jp-ii_apl_20010106_novo-millennio-ineunte.html.

207. Francis, *Evangelii Gaudium* (Boston: Pauline Books & Media, 2013), 152.

208. Kowalska, *Diary of St. Faustina*, para. 481.

CHAPTER 8

Like Lions Breathing Fire: Saint John Chrysostom

Let us then return from that table like lions breathing fire.

JOHN CHRYSOSTOM,
HOMILIES ON THE GOSPEL OF SAINT JOHN

EUCHARISTIC AMAZEMENT, AS WE have seen, has taken different forms in the lives of Catholics throughout history. We have explored two important witnesses: Saint Teresa of Avila and Saint Faustina Kowalska. Teresa taught us about Jesus' powerful personal presence in the Eucharist, and Faustina shared with us her experiences of the unique graces made present throughout the liturgical year. In this chapter we will be guided by a third saint, John Chrysostom. Chrysostom expressed his Eucharistic amazement in striking language. "Awesome in truth are the mysteries of the Church," he wrote, "awesome in truth is the altar."[209] Thus, it is fitting to conclude our reflections by turning to the Eucharistic teaching of Saint John Chrysostom, the Doctor of the Eucharist.

His Life

John Chrysostom was born in 347 in Antioch in modern-day Turkey. As a young man he felt called to monastic life and lived for about eight years as a hermit. He was then ordained a deacon in 381 and a priest in 386. His bishop recognized his gift for preaching, and from 386 to 398 he delivered exegetical homilies on many books of the Bible, including Genesis, the Gospels of Matthew and John, and Saint Paul's Letters to the Romans, Galatians, and Corinthians. His preaching established him as one of the Church's greatest expositors and earned him the name of Chrysostom, "golden mouthed." In 398 he reluctantly accepted an appointment as the Patriarch of Constantinople and zealously devoted himself to reform. His honesty, simplicity of life, and forthrightness earned him many powerful enemies, including the Empress Eudoxia. He was removed from office and sent into exile. He died in 407 while being forced to travel on foot in severe weather. His last words were "Glory be to God for all things." Saint John Chrysostom's feast day is September 13.

Because of "the vastness and depth of his teaching on the Most Holy Sacrament,"[210] Saint John is known as the Doctor of the Eucharist. He never flagged in his zeal to share with others the power and mystery of the Eucharist. In one of his homilies, he told his flock that "it is necessary to understand the marvel of the mysteries [the Eucharist]: what they are, why they are given and how they are profitable."[211] That understanding is as necessary today as it was in John's day. In this chapter John will open up for us the Old Testament events and persons that prefigured the Eucharist, the Mass as a participation in the heavenly liturgy, the Mass as a sacrifice, the fruits of Communion, the relationship between Communion and mercy, and the importance of worthy reception of Holy Communion.

A Type of Things to Come

John frequently explained the Eucharistic mystery by using *typology*; that is, he cited Old Testament persons and events that anticipated the Eucharist in different ways. As we saw in Chapter 2, the Church calls this method of interpretation typology. John explained typology to his flock in his commentary on the Last Supper (see Mt 26:28). John asked:

> Why can it have been that he ordained this sacrament then, at the time of the Passover? That you might learn from everything, both that he is the lawgiver of the Old Testament, and that the things there are foreshadowed because of these things. Therefore, I say, where the type is, there he puts the truth.[212]

In the Old Testament we encounter types; in Christ we encounter the fulfillment.

A dramatic example of John's typological interpretation is his explanation of the invocation of the Holy Spirit upon the

bread and wine—the *epiclesis*—in his book, *On the Priesthood*.
John saw this prefigured in Elijah's encounter with the prophets of Baal recounted in 1 Kings 18. Elijah and the prophets
of Baal each prepared a young bull as an offering and placed it
on wood. Elijah then told them, "Then you call on the name
of your god and I will call on the name of the LORD; the god
who answers by fire is indeed God" (v. 24). The prophets of
Baal prayed to Baal to consume the sacrifice which they had
prepared, but the sky was silent. Then it was Elijah's turn.
"Picture Elijah and the vast multitude standing around him,"
Chrysostom tells us, "and the sacrifice laid upon the altar of
stones, and all the rest of the people hushed into a deep silence
while the prophet alone offers up prayer: then the sudden
rush of fire from heaven upon the sacrifice—these are marvelous things, charged with terror."

This, says Chrysostom, is a figure of what takes place in
Mass: "Now then pass from this scene to the rites which are
celebrated in the present day; they are not only marvelous to
behold, but transcendent in terror." Just as Elijah called down
fire from heaven on the sacrifice, so the priest invokes the
Holy Spirit on the bread and wine:

> There stands the priest, not bringing down fire from
> heaven, but the Holy Spirit: and he makes prolonged sup-
> plication, not that some flame sent down from on high
> may consume the offerings, but that grace descending on
> the sacrifice may thereby enlighten the souls of all, and ren-
> der them more refulgent than silver purified by fire.

The sacramental reality amazes Chrysostom. "Who can
despise this most awe-inspiring mystery, unless he is stark

mad and senseless? Or do you not know that no human soul could have endured that fire in the sacrifice, but everyone present would have been utterly consumed, had not the assistance of God's grace been great?"[213]

John Chrysostom used another Old Testament type to explain the power of Christ's Blood—Israel's deliverance from Egypt. On the night of the Exodus, God commanded the Israelites to sacrifice an unblemished male lamb and "take some of the blood and put it on the two doorposts and the lintel of the houses" (Ex 12:7). "For the LORD will pass through to strike down the Egyptians; when he sees the blood on the lintel and on the two doorposts, the LORD will pass over that door and will not allow the destroyer to enter your houses to strike you down" (v. 23). If blood "had such great power . . . in the midst of Egypt, when smeared on the doorposts, much more the reality. . . . If death so shuddered at the shadow, tell me how would it not have dreaded the very reality?"[214]

What, then, is the power of Christ's Blood in our lives?

This Blood is the salvation of our souls; by it the soul is cleansed; by it, beautified; by it, inflamed. It makes our mind brighter than fire, it renders our soul more brilliant than gold. This Blood has been poured forth and has made heaven accessible.[215]

Old Testament types also anticipated the surpassing excellence of Christ's presence in the Eucharist: the tablets of stone with the Ten Commandments, the ark of the covenant, Aaron's rod, the manna in the wilderness, and the cherubim. These are all immeasurably surpassed by the Body and Blood of Christ. "It is not the cherubim you have, but the very Lord of the cherubim dwelling within, not jar or manna, or tablets of stone, or Aaron's rod, but the Lord's Body and Blood, and Spirit instead of letter, and grace surpassing human reason, and indescribable gift."[216] The Old Testament signs and rituals have been fulfilled by Christ, far surpassing the ancient signs. "Now, you are deemed the more deserving of greater symbols and awesome mysteries, the more you can demonstrate greater holiness."[217] For Chrysostom, Christ's Eucharistic presence compels us to pursue holiness. "Consider the degree of holiness required of the one receiving far greater symbols than the holy of holies received at that time."[218]

Join the Powers of Heaven

The last book of the Bible, the Revelation to the Apostle John, describes the worship ceaselessly celebrated in heaven: angels and the hosts of heaven singing songs of praise before One seated on a resplendent throne and the Lamb, an altar, incense rising from a gold censer, and saints robed in white (see chapters 4, 5, 7, and 8). The Church has always understood that the celebration of Mass is a participation in this heavenly liturgy. Chrysostom possessed a keen sacramental vision of this aspect of the liturgy. To those about to participate in Mass he said, "Reflect upon whom it is that you are near and with whom you are about to invoke God—the cherubim. Think of the choirs you are about to enter." Although we, unlike the angels, are "vested with a body," we "have been judged worthy to join the powers of heaven in singing the praises of him who is Lord of all."[219]

As an example of our participation in the heavenly liturgy at Mass, Chrysostom cited the Holy, Holy, Holy (the Sanctus), the song of the seraphim described in Isaiah 6:2–3 and Revelation 4:8 that concludes the Preface. "In heaven . . . the seraphim are singing: Holy, Holy, Holy," he wrote; "here on earth the same song resounds from countless human lips. The same praise of God resounds in heaven and on earth, one and the same hymn of thanksgiving, a song of jubilee, a chorus of joy." When the assembly joins the heavenly chorus in singing the Holy, Holy, Holy, each member is joined to the heavenly host. "You have joined the chorus of the seraphim, you are ranked as a citizen of the commonwealth above, you have been enrolled in the choir of Angels, you have conversed with the Lord, you have been in the company of Christ."[220]

Christ's presence on the altar following the Consecration is another moment that draws together heaven and earth. "At such a time angels stand by the priest; and the whole sanctuary, and the space around the altar is filled with the powers of heaven, in honor of him who is present on the altar."[221] At this moment in the Mass, the earthly assembly unites with angels and archangels in praise, offering, and intercession.

> It is not only men who raise this cry filled with holy awe, but the angels prostrate themselves before the Lord, the archangels pray to him. . . . Just as men cut palm branches and wave them before their kings to move them to think of love and mercy, so at this moment the angels present the very Body of their Lord as if it were a palm branch and they pray to him for all humanity.[222]

John Chrysostom opens our eyes to the full reality of this moment of the Mass—"Look, I entreat: a royal table is set before you, angels minister at that table, the King himself is there."[223]

John was left awestruck by the wonder of this moment, as he told his friend, Saint Basil the Great.

> For when you see the Lord sacrificed, and laid upon the altar, and the priest standing and praying over the Victim, and all the worshippers empurpled with that precious Blood, can you then think that you are still among men and standing upon the earth? Are you not, on the contrary, straightway translated to heaven, and casting out every carnal thought from the soul, do you not with disembodied spirit and pure reason contemplate the things which are in heaven? Oh! what a marvel! what love of God to man! He who sits on high with the Father is at that hour held in the hands of all, and gives himself to those who are willing to embrace and grasp him. And this all do through the eyes of faith![224]

John had a deep awareness of the hidden spiritual realities of the Mass. During Mass heaven descends to earth and earth ascends to heaven.

The Sacrifice Is One

The Eucharist, said John, is "this most awe-inspiring Mystery."[225] However, John was a perceptive and compassionate pastor, and he knew that his listeners might struggle to understand how the Mass is a sacrifice. Intrinsic to John's understanding of the Mass as a sacrifice is the concept of "memorial"— every celebration of the Eucharist "commemorates Christ's Passover, and it is *made present*: the sacrifice Christ offered once for all on the cross *remains ever present*" (CCC 1364; italics added). Anticipating his flock's possible confusion, he posed three questions. First, he asked, "Do not we offer every day?" His answer? "We offer indeed, but making a remembrance of his death."[226] The Mass makes present the one unique sacrifice of Christ. "That we offer now also, which was then offered, which cannot be exhausted. This is done in remembrance of what was then done."[227]

John then posed a second question. "But how can it [the sacrifice] be one and not many?"[228] How can so many daily offerings in different places all be the memorial of Christ's one unique sacrifice on Calvary? John addressed this question in many homilies, and recent popes have quoted his explanation—a witness to the enduring truth and clarity of John Chrysostom's insight into this mystery. In a homily on First Corinthians, John explained the one enduring Body of Christ in a passage quoted by Pope Pius XII in *Mediator Dei*:

> Death has not destroyed this Body which was pierced by nails and scourged, . . . This is that Body which was once covered with Blood, pierced by a lance, from which issued saving fountains upon the world, one of Blood and the other of water . . . This Body he gave to us to keep and eat, as a mark of his intense love.[229]

In a homily on Second Timothy, John said that the sacrifice offered now by the priest is the same that Christ offered at the Last Supper and was subsequently offered by the apostles, a passage quoted by Saint Paul VI:

It is the same offering, no matter who offers it, be it Peter or Paul. It is the same one that Christ gave to his disciples and the same one that priests now perform: the latter is in no way inferior to the former, for it is not men who sanctify the latter, but he who sanctified the former. For just as the words which God spoke are the same as those that the priest now pronounces, so too the offering is the same.[230]

Saint John Paul II also cited John's teaching on this theme, quoting a passage from one of John's homilies on Hebrews: "We always offer the same Lamb, not one today and another tomorrow, but always the same one. For this reason the sacrifice is always only one. . . . Even now we offer that Victim who was once offered and who will never be consumed."[231] The Body that Christ offered first at the Last Supper, then on Calvary, and now in the Mass is one and the same.

John put a third question. "Since the offering is made in many places, are there many Christs?" John emphatically taught that Christ is in no way divided.

Christ is one everywhere, being complete here and complete there also, one Body. As then while offered in many places, he is one body and not many bodies; so also [he is] one sacrifice . . . that we offer now also, which was then offered, which cannot be exhausted. This is done in remembrance of what was then done. . . . For we always offer the same, not one sheep now and tomorrow another, but always the same thing: so that the sacrifice is one . . . or rather we perform a remembrance of a sacrifice.[232]

It is given, said John, "as a mark of his intense love."[233]

Nurturing Eucharistic Amazement

The Eucharistic Prayers in the Mass affirm that Christ present on the altar is the same sacrificial Victim whose death reconciled us to the Father (see Eucharistic Prayers I and III). The awesome reality of Christ's Eucharistic presence is signaled by an important shift that occurs in the Mass following the Our Father. Up to this point the prayers address the Father, but the prayers that follow the Our Father address Christ, including two prayers said by the entire assembly: the Lamb of God, who is Jesus (see Jn 1:29), and the "Lord, I am not worthy," the Roman centurion's request to Jesus to heal his servant (see Lk 7:6–7). Though both are so familiar that they can be recited without thinking, it is important to recognize that they are both petitions to Jesus—who is now present on the altar—for mercy, peace, and healing. At this moment, as you prepare to receive Jesus, you can silently add your own petitions for mercy, peace, and healing, and, in this way, enter more personally into sacramental communion with Christ—the eternal Word, incarnate of the Virgin Mary, crucified, resurrected, glorified, seated now with the Father, and substantially present in the Eucharist.

Nourishing the Nobility of Our Souls

John taught his flock that the reception of Christ's Body and Blood brings about many fruits. Because Communion is a true personal encounter, it deepens our friendship with Christ. "This is also what Christ has done in order to lead us into a closer friendship and to show us his love for us. He has allowed those who desire him not only to see him but even to touch, and eat him, and fix their teeth in his flesh and to embrace him and satisfy all their love."[234] Christ richly bestows his blessings on his friends. "The Blood of Christ renews in us the image of our King, it produces an indescribable beauty and does not allow the nobility of our souls to be destroyed but ceaselessly waters and nourishes them."[235]

Through Eucharistic Communion, said John, Christ also equips his friends with his strength and power. "This Blood," he said, "if rightly taken, drives away devils, and keeps them afar off from us, while it calls to us angels and the Lord of angels. For wherever they see the Lord's Blood, devils flee, and angels run together."[236] The Blood of Christ is a powerful weapon against the enemy.

> If you show him a tongue stained with the precious Blood, he will not be able to make a stand; if you show him your mouth all crimsoned and ruddy, cowardly beast that he is, he will run away. . . . Do you wish to learn from another source as well the strength of this Blood? Look from where it first flowed and where it had its source! It flowed down from the cross, from the Master's side.[237]

John offered this striking exhortation to those who have just received the Blood of Christ: "Let us then return from that table like lions breathing fire, having become terrible to the devil, ruminating on our Head and on the love that he has shown for us."[238]

Many members of John's flock approached Communion with little faith or knowledge. He responded with instruction, not criticism. Many, he stated, partake "of Christ's Body lightly and incidentally, from custom and ordinance, rather than from consideration and understanding."[239] He gently urged them to approach Communion, "not by habit or with formality," but with "sincerity and purity of spirit."[240] He encouraged them to remember the honor and dignity that God was bestowing on them. "When you see him placed before you," he said, "say to yourselves: 'By virtue of this Body I am no longer dust and ashes, I am no longer a prisoner, but free; by virtue of this, I hope in heaven, and to receive its goods, the inheritance of the angels, and to converse with Christ.'"[241] Know and believe that the reception of Christ's Body and Blood "makes earth become to you a heaven . . . the heaven of heavens. . . . For it is not angels, nor archangels, nor heavens and heavens of heavens, that I show you, but the very Lord and Owner of these."[242] The fact that both Pope Pius XII and Pope Benedict XVI quote this passage in their teaching indicates its enduring value.

Nurturing Eucharistic Amazement

Saint John Paul II wrote that the union of the earthly and heavenly liturgies is an aspect of the Mass that deserves greater attention (see EE 19). Saint John Chrysostom offers us a striking vision of this aspect of the Mass. He describes a choir of heavenly beings, angels in the sanctuary, angels gathering and devils fleeing, the faithful returning from Communion like roaring lions. The union of the heavenly and earthly liturgies is an invitation to be more attentive to key parts of the Mass. Here are suggestions and examples for developing an awareness that in participating at Mass we are truly participating in the heavenly liturgy.

- As you prepare for Mass, remember that you are preparing to join heavenly choirs in praising the Most Holy Trinity.

- When you say the Confiteor in the Penitential Rite, you ask not only your brothers and sisters to pray for you, but also the Blessed Virgin Mary, the angels, and the saints, who are also present there with you.

- The Prefaces conclude with references to different orders of heavenly beings present—angels, archangels, hosts and powers of heaven, thrones, and dominions, and this leads into the Holy, Holy, Holy, which is sung in union with the seraphim. You might also find enlightening the lists of these heavenly beings given in Eph 1:21 and Col 1:16.

✦ Chrysostom also emphasized the presence of angels around the altar after the Consecration, as well as when the faithful are returning from Communion.

✦ John Chrysostom's teaching on the powerful presence of angels at the Mass captures the imagination and deepens the faith of children. Using pictures of angels, demonstrate the actions of the angels at the various parts of the holy Sacrifice of the Mass, using the words of Chrysostom as a guide.

Become More Merciful

John Chrysostom also explained how Eucharistic Communion unites us to Christ and to one another. "What is bread?" he asked. "The Body of Christ." He continued, "And what does it become when we eat it? The Body of Christ; not many bodies but one Body." [243] John employed vivid images to explain our union with Christ: "He has mixed up himself with us. He has kneaded up his Body with ours."[244] "We are mingled with him, and become one Body and one flesh with Christ."[245] Christ makes us "one body and one flesh" with him "to show his love for us."[246] This intimate union with Christ is also union with one another. "Just as bread becomes one loaf although it is made of numerous grains of wheat . . . , so we too are united both with one another and with Christ."[247]

This in turn means that we should show others the love that Christ has shown us by uniting us to himself and to one another. "Now, if we are nourished by the same loaf and all become the same thing, why do we not also show the same love, so as to become one in this dimension, too?"[248]

John exhorted his flock on this point.

> You have tasted the Blood of the Lord, yet you do not recognize your brother. . . . You dishonor this table when you do not judge worthy of sharing your food someone judged worthy to take part in this meal. . . . God freed you from all your sins and invited you here, but you have not become more merciful. (CCC 1397)

So important is drawing mercy from the Eucharist that Saint John Paul II said, "Our concern for those in need . . . will be the criterion by which the authenticity of our Eucharistic celebrations is judged."[249]

Nurturing Eucharistic Amazement

Saint John Chrysostom gave voice to the Church's perennial desire to be the merciful Body of Christ. One of the ways she has encouraged her members to do so is by practicing the corporal and spiritual works of mercy. The corporal works of mercy are feeding the hungry, giving drink to the thirsty, clothing the naked, sheltering the homeless, visiting the sick and imprisoned, and burying the dead. The spiritual works of mercy are counseling the doubtful, instructing the ignorant, admonishing sinners, comforting the afflicted, forgiving offenses, bearing wrongs patiently, and praying for the living and the dead. After praying and reflecting on the spiritual and corporal works of mercy, choose one or two works of mercy to which you feel more especially drawn. Carry them out personally or through a parish ministry.

I Beseech, Beg, and Implore

Like Saint Teresa of Avila, John took seriously Saint Paul's warning to the Corinthians not to receive Communion unworthily and so bring judgment upon themselves. "Is this Table which is the cause of so many blessings and teeming with life, become judgment? Not from its own nature, says he, but from the will of him that approaches . . . the mysteries become provisions of greater punishment to such as partake unworthily."[250] In his encyclical *Ecclesia de Eucharistia*, Saint John Paul II quoted John Chrysostom's passionate appeal to his flock to prepare to receive the Eucharist worthily:

> I too raise my voice, I beseech, beg, and implore that no one draw near to this sacred table with a sullied and corrupt conscience. Such an act, in fact, can never be called "communion," not even were we to touch the Lord's Body

a thousand times over, but "condemnation," "torment" and "increase of punishment."[251]

The key is to see with the eyes of faith and knowledge the One who is before us. "For if you truly knew who it is that lies before you, and who he is that gives himself, and to whom, you will need no other evidence, but this is enough for you to use all vigilance."[252]

Conclusion

Saint John Chrysostom's comprehensive understanding of Christ's presence is striking and profound. On the altar is the One who fulfills and surpasses all the Old Testament figures and rites. On the altar is the One who unites heaven and earth, drawing to himself in praise and adoration all the heavenly host and transporting those present to the heavenly heights. On the altar is the One spotless Lamb, the pure sacrifice offered from east to west, the same Christ always and everywhere. On the altar is the One who unites us to himself and so to one another. On the altar is the One who beautifies and ennobles our soul. On the altar is the One who has shown us mercy so that we might be merciful, recognizing and loving him in the poor. On the altar is the One who has given us unfathomable blessings. On the altar is the One who offers life to all. May God give us eyes to see, minds to understand, and hearts to believe and adore.

Notes

209. John Chrysostom, *Homilies on the Gospel of St. John*, 14, 46.4.167.

210. Benedict XVI, "Angelus Discourse," September 18, 2005, The Holy See, Vatican.va. https://www.vatican.va/content/benedict-xvi/en/angelus/2005/documents/hf_ben-xvi_ang_20050918.html.

211. John Chrysostom, *Homilies on the Gospel of St. John*, 46.3.166.

212. John Chrysostom, *Homilies on the Gospel According to St. Matthew*, trans. Philip Schaff, NPNF 10 (Edinburgh: T&T Clark, 1993), 82.1.491.

213. John Chrysostom, *On the Priesthood*, trans. Philip Schaff, NPNF 9, Book III, 4:47.

214. John Chrysostom, *Homilies on the Gospel of St. John*, 14, 46.3.166–67.

215. John Chrysostom, *Homilies on the Gospel of St. John*, 14, 46.3.167.

216. John Chrysostom, *Commentary on the Psalms, Volume 2*, trans. with an introduction by Robert Charles Hill (Brookline, MA: Holy Cross Orthodox Press, 1998), 202. *Homily in Ps.* 134.2.

217. John Chrysostom, *Commentary on the Psalms, Volume 2*, 202. *Homily in Ps.* 134.2.

218. John Chrysostom, *Commentary on the Psalms, Volume 2*, 202. *Homily in Ps.* 134.2.

219. John Chrysostom, *On the Incomprehensible Nature of God* (Fathers of the Church 72), trans. Paul W. Harkins (Washington, DC: Catholic University of America Press, 1984), *Adv. Anom. Homily* 3, 113.

220. John Chrysostom, *On the Priesthood*, 9, Homily to those who had not attended the assembly 4.313.

221. John Chrysostom, *On the Priesthood*, 9, Book VI, 4:76.

222. John Chrysostom, *On the Incomprehensible Nature of God*, *Adv. Anom. Homily* 3, 113.

223. John Chrysostom, *Homilies on Ephesians*, trans. Philip Schaff, NPNF 13 (Edinburgh: T&T Clark, 1993), 3.

224. John Chrysostom, *On the Priesthood*, 9, Book III, 4:46.

225. John Chrysostom, *On the Priesthood*, 9, Book III, 4:47.

226. John Chrysostom, *Homilies on the Epistle to the Hebrews*, trans. Philip Schaff, NPNF 14 (Edinburgh: T&T Clark, 1993), 17.6.449.

227. John Chrysostom, *Homilies on the Epistle to the Hebrews*, 14, 17.6.449.

228. John Chrysostom, *Homilies on the Epistle to the Hebrews*, 14, 17.6.449.

229. Pius XII, *Mediator Dei*, 134 [*In I ad Cor.*, 24:4].

230. Paul VI, *Mysterium Fidei*, 38 [*Homily on the Second Epistle to Timothy* 2.4; PG 62.612].

231. John Paul II, *Ecclesia de Eucharistia*, 12 [*In Epistolam ad Hebraeos Homiliae, Hom.* 17,3: PG 63, 131].

232. John Chrysostom, *Homilies on the Epistle to the Hebrews*, 14, 17.6.449.

233. John Chrysostom, *Homilies on the Epistles of Paul to the Corinthians*, trans. Philip Schaff, NPNF 12 (Edinburgh: T&T Clark), 24.7.143.

234. John Chrysostom, *Homilies on the Gospel of St. John*, 14, 46.3.166.

235. Benedict XVI, "Letter of His Holiness Benedict XVI on the Occasion of the 16th Centenary of the Death of St. John Chrysostom," August 10, 2007, The Holy See, Vatican.va, 3.8 [Cf. Johannes Chrysostomus, *In Ioannem* 46, 3 (PG 63, 261)]. https://www.vatican.va/content/benedict-xvi/en/letters/2007/documents/hf_ben-xvi_let_20070810_giovanni-crisostomo.html.

236. John Chrysostom, *Homilies on the Gospel of St. John*, 14, 46.3.166.

237. John Chrysostom, *Baptismal Instructions* (Westminster, MD: The Newman Press, 1963), 60–61.

238. John Chrysostom, *Homilies on the Gospel of St. John*, 14, 46.3.166.

239. John Chrysostom, *Homilies on Ephesians*, 13, 3.164.

240. Benedict XVI, "Letter of His Holiness Benedict XVI," 3.8 [Cf. Johannes Chrysostomus, *In Epistulam ad Ephesios* 3, 4 (PG 62, 28). Cf. id., *In Epistulam i ad Corinthos* 24 (PG 61, 197–206); id., *In Epistulam i ad Corinthos* 27, 4 (PG 61, 229–30); id., *In Epistulam i ad Timotheum* 15, 4 (PG 62, 583–86); id., *In Matthaeum* 82, 6 (PG 58, 744–46)].

241. Benedict XVI, "Letter of His Holiness Benedict XVI," 3.8 [Cf. Johannes Chrysostomus, *In Epistulam i ad Corinthos* 24, 4 (PG 61, 203)].

242. John Chrysostom, *Homilies on the Epistles of Paul to the Corinthians*, 12, 24.8.143.

243. Benedict XVI, "Letter of His Holiness Benedict XVI," 3.6 [Cf. Johannes Chrysostomus, *In Epistulam i ad Corinthos* 24, 2 (PG 61, 200)].

244. John Chrysostom, *Homilies on the Gospel of St. John*, 14, 46.3.166.

245. John Chrysostom, *Homilies on the Gospel of St. Matthew*, trans. Philip Schaff, NPNF 10 (Edinburgh: T&T Clark, 1993), 82.5.495.

246. John Chrysostom, *Homilies on the Gospel of St. John*, 14, 46.3.166.

247. Benedict XVI, "Letter of His Holiness Benedict XVI," 3.6 [Cf. Johannes Chrysostomus, *In Epistulam i ad Corinthos* 24, 2 (PG 61, 200)].

248. Benedict XVI, "Letter of His Holiness Benedict XVI," 3.6 [Cf. Johannes Chrysostomus, *In Epistulam i ad Corinthos* 24, 2 (PG 61, 200)].

249. John Paul II, *Mane Nobiscum Domine* (Vatican City: Libreria Editrice Vaticana, Vatican Press, 2004), 28.

250. John Chrysostom, *Homilies on the Epistles of Paul to the Corinthians*, 12, 28.2.164.

251. John Paul II, *Ecclesia de Eucharistia*, 36 [Saint John Chrysostom, *Homiliae in Isaiam*, 6, 3: PG 56, 139].

252. John Chrysostom, *Homilies on the Epistles of Paul to the Corinthians*, 12, 28.2.164.

CHAPTER 9

Living Eucharistic Amazement

Amazement seized all of them.

LUKE 5:26

T HE JOURNEY WE HAVE taken to understand and cultivate *a sense of awe, love, and childlike trust in the goodness
and power of the Eucharistic Christ and a desire never to be
parted from him* is almost complete. We have one final question to consider: How does Eucharistic amazement change
us? To answer this question, we will turn now to people whose
amazing encounters with Jesus have been recorded in the
Gospels: How did they respond? What did they do? And
since Eucharistic amazement is also the fruit of profound
encounters with Jesus, what can these people teach us?

Be with Him

The first response of many of those who encountered Jesus was a desire to stay with him. After Jesus had freed a man from a legion of demons, he begged to be with Jesus (see Mk 5:18). The Samaritans from the village of the woman at the well went to Jesus and asked him to stay with them (see Jn 4:40). And while the two disciples on the road to Emmaus did not recognize Jesus as he talked to them on the road, their hearts were strangely warmed, and they asked him to stay and share a meal with them (see Lk 24:29). Eucharistic amazement inspires in us that same fervent desire to be with Jesus.

We have already explored some options for remaining with Jesus. The preeminent way is spending time with Jesus at Mass and after Communion. And if circumstances allow, this can be prolonged by prayer after Mass. I still remember being at the Catholic Center at Texas A&M University for a weekday Mass that was attended by about 200 students. When Mass ended, no one left. Without prompting or instruction, everyone knelt and prayed. Another possibility is to spend time with the Lord through *lectio divina*. It too is an encounter with Christ because he is present in his word.

Spending time with Jesus in Eucharistic Adoration, either in prayer before the tabernacle or during Eucharistic Exposition, can be a powerful experience. Check the schedule in your parish: When is the church open for prayer? Does the parish offer Exposition and Benediction of the Blessed Sacrament? Consider spending an hour with Jesus in a Eucharistic Adoration chapel.

Serving as a liturgical minister is another possibility of being with Jesus and helping others encounter him, in his word as a reader, in the Eucharist as an extraordinary minister of Holy Communion, and in the people gathered in his name as an usher or greeter. Finally, in the parable of the sheep and goats (see Mt 25:31–46), Jesus taught us that he is present in those in need. If your parish offers social ministry programs, consider volunteering. Discerning Jesus' presence in the Eucharist assists us in discerning the other ways he is present within and outside of Mass.

Tell Others about Him

Those who experienced a transforming encounter with Jesus had to tell others about him. Immediately after the annunciation, the Blessed Virgin Mary hurried to visit and rejoice with Elizabeth, who was pregnant with John the Baptist (see Lk 1:39–46). When the prophetess Anna saw the infant Jesus in the Temple with his parents and Simeon, she immediately began telling others about him (see Lk 2:38). The leper whom Jesus cured with a word and a touch, even though he had been warned by Jesus to keep silent about what had happened, began to tell everyone about him (see Mk 1:44–45).

There are a variety of ways that you can tell others about Christ's wondrous presence in the Eucharist. One quiet but effective way is your attitude at Mass, the reverence and attention with which you listen, make the responses, and pray. You never know who will be inspired and touched by your example. My experiences as a teacher, especially in a Communist country, and as a priest have taught me the value of personal witness. People are looking for Jesus and want to see him in someone like them. You can also talk to family, friends, fellow parishioners, and colleagues about him, trusting the Lord to prompt questions and to open doors and hearts (see Col 4:3). The Mass itself urges us to do this when we are dismissed with the words, "Go and announce the Gospel of the Lord."253

Come and See

People who encountered Jesus not only told others about him, they also invited them to see for themselves. As soon as Andrew met Jesus, he told his brother Peter and took him to meet Jesus (see Jn 1:40–42). When the disciples interrupted Jesus' conversation with the woman at the well, she returned home and urged the people to see for themselves the man who had told her so much about herself (see Jn 4:27–30). As Jesus' fame grew, others sought him out. Following Palm Sunday, Greeks in Jerusalem for the Passover came to Philip and gave voice to the deepest desire of every heart, then and now: "We wish to see Jesus" (Jn 12:21). People like to be asked—a personal invitation is often more meaningful and effective than a general appeal. So invite others to meet Jesus at Mass, in Eucharistic Adoration, in a Bible study, or in a ministry to those in need. Invite them to come and see him for themselves.

Live Generously

Some who encountered Jesus' generous welcome responded with generosity. Zacchaeus, a rich but hated chief tax collector, climbed a tree to see Jesus. Zacchaeus was stunned when Jesus, shocking the crowd, announced that he was coming to his home (see Lk 19:1–10). Overwhelmed, Zacchaeus immediately offered half of his wealth to the poor and repaid fourfold those he had cheated. His generosity mirrors the abundant generosity of Jesus. At the wedding in Cana, Jesus changed the water of six stone jars, each containing twenty to thirty gallons, into wine (see Jn 2:1–11)! After the five thousand had eaten and were satisfied, twelve baskets of food were left (see Mk 6:43), and after feeding the four thousand, there were still seven baskets of food (see Mk 8:8). In these cases Jesus went far beyond what was needed. Experiencing Eucharistic amazement inspires a similar generosity in us, demonstrated in the time we give to the Lord and to his people, in the sharing of our talents, and in our generous giving according to and even beyond our means (see 2 Cor 8:3). When we have a profound sense of Eucharistic amazement we know that there is no limit to God's generosity.

Give Thanks

A life aflame with Eucharistic amazement overflows with thanksgiving. When Jesus healed the ten lepers, nine hurried away (a cautionary reminder to us!), but one came back and fell at his feet in praise and thanksgiving (see Lk 17:16). The Mass itself teaches us the importance of being thankful. Every preface begins with an exhortation to give thanks because it is "right and just, our duty and our salvation, always and everywhere to give you thanks."[254] You might consider using this familiar phrase for *lectio divina*, carefully savoring each word—*right, just, our duty, our salvation, always, everywhere*. A heart rich in Eucharistic amazement leads us to a life of thankfulness. One of the dismissals that concludes the Mass exhorts: "Go in peace, glorifying the Lord by your life."[255]

Guard This Gift

The Apostle Paul exhorted Timothy to guard what the Holy Spirit had entrusted to him (see 1 Tim 6:20; 2 Tim 1:14), and it is an apt exhortation to us as well, for we, like Timothy, are subject to the enticements of the world and the opposition of a prowling adversary. Reflection on the fruits of Eucharistic amazement will help us be good stewards of the great treasure entrusted to us. We can ask ourselves questions such as: Am I spending regular time with our Eucharistic Lord? Am I speaking to others about him? Am I inviting them to come and see for themselves? Am I growing in generosity and thankfulness? Am I growing in love? Asking and honestly answering these questions on a regular basis will ensure that we are growing in a spirit of Eucharistic amazement and helping to enkindle it in others.

Let us together press on with great faith and love to meet the Lord in the Mass and add our voices to the great symphony of Eucharistic amazement. Let us exclaim with Saint Teresa of Avila, "Oh, what a good God! Oh, how good a Lord and how powerful!"[256]

A Prayer before the Eucharistic Lord

I love you, Jesus, my Eucharistic Lord.
You are my light, my joy, and my peace.
I come to abide with you
so that I may become like you:
merciful and forgiving,
humble and gentle,
patient and loving,
generous and thankful.
Be with me always.
Thank you, Jesus, for your indescribable gift!

Notes

253. *Roman Missal*, Order of Mass 144.

254. *Roman Missal*, Order of Mass (Preface I of Advent) 33.

255. *Roman Missal*, Order of Mass 144.

256. Teresa of Avila, *Collected Works*, 1:221.

Acknowledgments

The author and Pauline Books & Media gratefully acknowledge the following sources from which excerpts appear in this book:

Papal and magisterial texts copyright © Dicastero per la Comunicazione–Libreria Editrice Vaticana. All rights reserved. Used with permission.

Excerpts from the English translation of *Lectionary for Mass* © 1969, 1981, 1997, International Commission on English in the Liturgy Corporation (ICEL); excerpts from the English translation of *The Roman Missal* © 2010, ICEL. All rights reserved.

Excerpts from the *General Instruction on the Roman Missal* © 2003, United States Catholic Conference of Bishops Inc. Washington, DC. All rights reserved.

Excerpts from the *Diary*, by Saint Faustina Kowalska, used with permission of the Marian Fathers of the Immaculate Conception of the Blessed Virgin Mary. Stockbridge, MA.

Excerpts from *Guigo II: The Ladder of Monks: A Letter on the Contemplative Life and Twelve Meditations*, copyright © 1979 by Edmund Colledge and James Walsh. All rights reserved. The work of Cistercian Publications is made possible in part by support from Western Michigan University to the Institute of Cistercian Studies. Published by arrangement with Doubleday & Company, Inc. Used with permission.

Excerpts from *The Collected Works of Teresa of Avila, Volume One, The Collected Works of Teresa of Avila, Volume Two, Collected Works of Saint John of the Cross*, and *Story of a Soul: The Autobiography of Saint Thérèse of Lisieux*, 3rd ed. used with permission of ICS Publications. Washington, DC.

Excerpts from *The Liturgical Year*, Volume 1, (Advent), Volume 2, (Christmas Bk 1) by Prosper Guéranger, used with permission of Loreto Publications, PO Box 603, Fitzwilliam, NH 03447.

The publisher apologizes for any errors or omissions in the above list and would be grateful if notified of any corrections that should be incorporated in future reprints or editions of this book.

Further Reading

Benedict XVI. *Sacramentum Caritatis* (*The Sacrament of Charity*), Boston: Pauline Books & Media, 2007.

Pope Benedict XVI wrote this to renew fervor and enthusiasm for the Eucharist. He discusses the Eucharist under three headings: "A Mystery to Be Believed," "A Mystery to Be Celebrated," and "A Mystery to Be Lived." It is a wonderful overview of almost every aspect of the Eucharist.

Raniero Cantalamessa. *The Eucharist: Our Sanctification*, rev. ed., Collegeville: Liturgical Press, 1995.

Cardinal Cantalamessa was a professor of the history of early Christianity until his appointment as the Preacher to the Papal Household by Saint John Paul II in 1980 and was confirmed in this position by Benedict XVI and Francis. I find this book particularly valuable for its many selections from the Fathers of the Church.

Congregation for Divine Worship and the Discipline of the Sacraments. *Directory on Popular Piety and the Liturgy*, Vatican City, 2001.

This is a very useful and practical resource. For this book I drew on Chapter 4: "The Liturgical Year and Popular Piety." The reader may also find the chapters on the Blessed Virgin Mary and the saints and blesseds helpful. The document can be accessed on the Vatican website.

John Paul II. *Ecclesia de Eucharistia* (*On the Eucharist in Its Relationship to the Church*), Boston: Pauline Books & Media, 2003.

This is Saint John Paul II's last encyclical on the Eucharist, written to correct errors in doctrine and practice and to rekindle Eucharistic amazement. For my book I relied primarily on the Introduction and the first two chapters.

Maria Faustina Kowalska. *Diary of Saint Maria Faustina Kowalska: Divine Mercy in My Soul*, Stockbridge: Marian Press, 2012.

Of particular interest is Saint Faustina's account of the revelation and description of the Image of Divine Mercy (nos. 47–49, 299) and the Chaplet of Divine Mercy (no. 476). She also wrote two beautiful litanies, the Litany to the Blessed Host (no. 356) and the Litany to Divine Mercy (no. 949).

Teresa of Avila. *The Collected Works of Teresa of Avila*, trans. Kieran Kavanaugh and Otilio Rodriguez, Vol. 1, *The Book of Her Life, Spiritual Testimonies, Soliloquies*, and Vol. II, *The Way of Perfection, Meditations on the Song of Songs, The Interior Castle*, Washington, DC: ICS Publications, 1980.

The Book of Her Life is a good introduction to Saint Teresa's life and spirituality. The same volume includes her *Spiritual Testimonies*, many of which discuss specific experiences she had during or after Mass. *The Way of Perfection* is a commentary on the Our Father. She discusses the Eucharist in depth in Chapter 34 on the petition for our daily bread.

Thomas à Kempis. *The Imitation of Christ*.

This beloved spiritual classic is divided into four sections: Counsels on the Spiritual Life, Counsels on the Inner Life, On Inward Consolation, and On the Blessed Sacrament. It is available in a number of editions.

Francis-Xavier Nguyen Van Thuan. *Five Loaves and Two Fish*, Boston: Pauline Books & Media, 2003.

This is a short book of seven chapters, the first five titled Loaves and the last two titled Fish. The Fourth Loaf is "The Eucharist: My Only Strength," but there are references to the Eucharist throughout the book.

Robert Louis Wilken. *The Spirit of Early Christian Thought: Seeking the Face of God*, New Haven: Yale University Press, 2003.

This is an excellent introduction to the thought and spirituality of the Church Fathers written for a general audience by a renowned scholar. He discusses the Eucharist in Chapter 2, "An Awesome and Unbloody Sacrifice."

Reflection Questions

Chapter 1
Does God Act Today?

1. Have I ever thought about how God is acting in the world? Have I ever heard or read about how God acts in the Mass? What do I expect to happen at Mass?

2. Do I consider the Mass to be a personal meeting with God my Father in Christ and the Holy Spirit? Am I attracted by the description of the Mass as a personal meeting with God my Father in Christ and the Holy Spirit?

3. How would I describe the Mass to a non-Catholic?

4. Before reading this chapter, how would I have described Christ's presence in the Eucharist? How has my understanding changed after reading the explanation that the Eucharist is *the substantial presence of Christ's glorified body under the appearances of bread and wine and discerned by faith*?

5. Which of the six examples of Eucharistic amazement (Abitene martyrs, Saint Augustine, Saint Francis of Assisi, Saint Thomas Aquinas, Saint Thérèse of Lisieux, Venerable Francis-Xavier Nguyen Van Thuan) spoke to me most? Why?

6. What are the most powerful moments of the Mass for me? Why?

7. What in this chapter was most illuminating?

8. How has my understanding of Communion been enriched?*

*Space for personal notes can be found following page 183.

Chapter 2
Power Came Forth from Him

1. How have I experienced Jesus' concern and care for me? Which aspects of Jesus' healing of the woman were new to me?

2. Which liturgical signs are most familiar to me? Have I experienced God working through liturgical signs? If so, which ones, and how?

3. Had I ever thought about how each Person of the Trinity works in the Mass?

4. What most attracts me about the working of each Person of the Trinity?

5. What situations are most challenging for my faith?

6. Which of the three ways of increasing my faith most appeal to me? Why?

7. How have I experienced love as a way of knowing others? God?

Chapter 3
Christ Himself Is Present: Saint Teresa of Avila

1. Saint Teresa described how the vision she received of Christ's glory changed her understanding of Communion. How has it changed the way I understand and approach Communion?

2. Have I ever experienced healing, relief, or comfort after receiving Communion? If so, how?

3. How can Teresa's experiences strengthen my faith in the power of the Eucharist?

4. Have I ever experienced a powerful encounter with a saint (or saints) during Mass? If so, how would I describe it?

5. Have I ever experienced some sort of guidance or direction after Communion, or at another point during Mass? If not, after reading about Teresa's experiences am I more likely to ask the Lord for guidance during Mass?

6. Teresa received deeper insights about the faith during Mass. Have I ever received such insights? If so, which ones?

7. What aspects of the Christian faith am I most interested in? In what areas is my faith seeking understanding?

8. How do I spend the time immediately after receiving Communion? Do I ever experience distractions? If so, how do I deal with them?

9. How strong is my desire to receive the Eucharist? What strengthens my desire? What weakens my desire?

10. How often do I go to Confession? Do I regularly make an examination of conscience, reflecting on my relationship with God and my neighbor?

Chapter 4
The Mass: The Renewal of the Covenant

1. Have I ever heard or thought about the Mass as a renewal of the Covenant? How did I understand the phrase "the new and eternal covenant" in the Consecration?

2. What was my reaction when I read that the Mass draws us into the compelling love of Christ and sets us on fire? Have I experienced that?

3. Which image of the Covenant—a father and child, a husband and wife, a shepherd and his flock—attracts me most? Why?

4. How has learning about the Last Supper as a fulfilment of the Mosaic Covenant changed my thinking about the Mass?

5. Has the explanation of the different Old Testament types fulfilled by Christ broadened my understanding of the Mass? Of Christ? Of Sacred Scripture? If so, how?

6. What effect will this chapter have on my participation in the Mass?

7. Has this chapter deepened my understanding of how the Mass is the work of the Trinity? If so, how?

Chapter 5
Christ's Mysteries Made Present

1. Which figure or source in this chapter spoke to me the most—Prosper Guéranger, Pius Parsch, Pope Pius XII, Vatican Council II, or the *Catechism of the Catholic Church*? What attracted me in particular?

2. Each celebration of the Mass makes present unique graces. Is this a new concept for me? How might it affect the way I prepare for and participate in the Mass?

3. What was my reaction to the teaching on the work of the Holy Spirit in the Mass? Have I personally experienced this?

4. Do I experience the events celebrated in the Mass as happening now?

5. What did this chapter contribute to my understanding of Eucharistic amazement?

Chapter 6
His Divine Love Provides: Saint Faustina

1. What was my initial reaction to the extraordinary graces that Saint Faustina received, graces such as locutions, physical suffering, and visions? Did I experience any hesitations or doubt? Did her experiences strengthen my own faith and expectations?

2. Which of Saint Faustina's experiences particularly stand out to me? Why?

3. How can Saint Faustina's experiences with the Blessed Virgin Mary strengthen my devotion to our Lady?

4. Has this chapter added to my understanding of how all three Persons of the Trinity are active during Mass? If so, how?

5. Has Saint Faustina's witness changed my understanding of the mercy of God? If so, how?

6. How might Faustina's intense prayer life deepen my own prayer life?

7. Both Saint Teresa of Avila and Saint Faustina experienced extraordinary graces during Mass. Which saint attracted me more? Why?

8. How can Faustina's experiences help me experience more deeply the "today" of the Mass?

Chapter 7
Preparing for Mass

1. Which variable part(s) of the Mass discussed in this chapter am I less familiar with? More familiar with? Which am I most likely to use to prepare for Mass? Which might I use in my own prayer life?

2. What has been my experience of *lectio divina*? Which part(s) of the Mass do I feel drawn to use for *lectio divina*?

3. When and how do I prepare for Mass? Will I make any changes after reading this chapter?

4. How has preparing for Mass changed my participation in Mass?

Chapter 8
Like Lions Breathing Fire: Saint John Chrysostom

1. Have I ever heard or read about the Mass joining the eternal worship in heaven? If not, what was my initial reaction?

2. What would be different if I began to see the Mass the way that Saint John Chrysostom saw it?

3. How has John influenced the way I view the liturgical signs—altar, gestures, colors, words? Has he helped me pass from the visible signs to the invisible realities they bear?

4. How has John's use of Old Testament typology changed my understanding of the Mass? Which of his Old Testament types especially attracted me? Why?

5. Which of John's quotes particularly struck me? Which am I most likely to remember? Why?

6. What has John contributed to my own Eucharistic amazement?

7. How might this chapter change my participation in Mass?

Chapter 9
Living Eucharistic Amazement

1. Which of the responses discussed in this chapter (Be with Him, Tell Others about Him, Come and See, Live Generously, Give Thanks) have I experienced? Which do I most want to experience?

2. What do I personally need to do, what changes do I need to make, to guard my Eucharistic amazement?

3. How has my *sense of awe, love, and childlike trust in the goodness and power of the Eucharistic Christ, and my desire never to be parted from him*, grown through reading this book? What has been most helpful? Most memorable?

4. What chapters or sections am I most likely to reread? To share with others? Why?

5. How has my participation in the Mass changed as a result of reading this book?

Pauline
BOOKS & MEDIA

A mission of the Daughters of St. Paul

As apostles of Jesus Christ,
evangelizing today's world:

We are CALLED to holiness
by God's living Word and Eucharist.

We COMMUNICATE the Gospel message
through our lives and through all
available forms of media.

We SERVE the Church
by responding to the hopes and needs
of all people with the Word of God,
in the spirit of St. Paul.

For more information visit us at:
www.pauline.org